What People Are Saying About
Gossip . . .

"Everyone will find inspiration and guidance in this wonderful work on the discipline of speech. With remarkable clarity and order, Lori and Bob have taken a complex subject and made it accessible and engaging to read."

Rebbetzin Faygie Twersky

"Lori and Bob do directly address the issue of gossip, but from a perspective that is of broader and deeper importance: kindness and respect for others. This is a thought-provoking book that will help you establish healthier relationships with others and, in so doing, with yourself. The wonderful quotations, relevant passages from scripture and lively stories illustrate simple different pathways to being the person you want to be."

Mark Albion, Ph.D.
author, *Making a Life, Making a Living*®
www.makingalife.com

"Lori and Bob will be richly rewarded for the effort they have given to this work. You cannot help but internalize this powerful book, and as you do, your life improves dramatically. It will help anyone eliminate a very destructive habit they very likely inherited at birth. I will recommend it in every seminar I conduct, and you will find it on our Web sites."

Bob Proctor
chairman, LifeSuccess Productions

"Every page of this book has information that can enhance a person's life. A great idea would be for readers to use these chapters as an actual program to upgrade their awareness of avoiding gossip."

Rabbi Moshe Goldberger
author, *Master Your Thoughts* and *Be a Friend*

"There is no other subject that demands to be spoken and examined than gossip. It has ruined lives, assassinated personalities, split families, alienated friends and has even caused murder. Bob Burg and Lori Palatnik have bravely and successfully confronted this evil. Using Biblical and secular writings, they show from the beginning of time that others have addressed this common problem of all ages. From Moses, the Prophets, David and Solomon, we have warnings and admonishments about gossip. Bob and Lori have pulled off the excuses we try to hide behind. However, they do not stop there. They give practical, workable and daily suggestions to overcome and break the habit of speaking evil of others. This book does not belong in your library; it belongs on your bed stand for daily reading!"

The Reverend Dr. Earl Bailey

"If you are shooting for harmony in your relationships and integrity in your life, then this is the book for you. A must-read."

David J. Lieberman, Ph.D.
renowned behaviorist and author,
Make Peace with Anyone (St. Martin's Press)

"A beautiful book, a must-read for everyone. It took only a few pages for me to ask God to forgive me."

Charles "T" Jones
author, *Life Is Tremendous*

"Just as 'many are called, but few are chosen,' many books are written, but few have impacted my life as much as *Gossip*. It will cause you to take a serious look at your speech and how your words can literally destroy not only relationships, but individuals as well. The path to greater happiness, by eliminating harmful discussions from your daily conversations, will literally jump off the pages for you as it did for me."

Jim "Gymbeaux" Brown
team leader and broker,
Keller Williams Realty

"Gossip is one of those things, like smoking, that you know you need to quit—you just need to be empowered as to how! This book drives home the value of reducing nonproductive talk from our lives. This is a first step to living a positive life. As the Dalai Lama says, 'You don't have to be a God, just stop hurting people.'"

Tim Sanders
author, *Love Is the Killer App:
How to Win Business and Influence Friends*

"Ralph Waldo Emerson once said that speech is power, a concept explored in Lori Palatnik and Bob Burg's insightful little book *Gossip: Ten Pathways to Eliminate It from Your Life and Transform Your Soul*. The authors discuss the role of lashon hora (evil speech) in the Bible and in Jewish tradition, exploring the immediate—and even the eternal—consequences of negative gossip. The book is accessible and well-designed, with powerful pull-out quotes from sources as diverse as Maimonides and Henry Ward Beecher, all illustrating the destructive power of evil words."

Publishers Weekly

GOSSIP

TEN PATHWAYS TO ELIMINATE IT FROM YOUR LIFE AND TRANSFORM YOUR SOUL

Lori Palatnik
with Bob Burg

SiMCHA
PRESS
An Imprint of Health Communications, Inc.®

Deerfield Beach, Florida
www.simchapress.com

Library of Congress Cataloging-in-Publication Data

Palatnik, Lori.
    Gossip : ten pathways to eliminate it from your life and transform your soul /
Lori Palatnik ; with Bob Burg.
      p.   cm.
    Includes bibliographical references.
    ISBN 0-7573-0055-3
    1. Gossip. 2. Libel and slander—Religious aspects—Judaism.
3. Ethics, Jewish. I. Burg, Bob. II. Title.

BJ1535.G6 P35 2002
296.3'672—dc21

                                       2002070806

©2002 Lori Palatnik and Bob Burg
ISBN 0-7573-0055-3 (trade paper)

Simcha Press, its Logos and Marks are trademarks of Health Communications, Inc.

Publisher: Simcha Press
                An Imprint of Health Communications, Inc.
                3201 S.W. 15th Street
                Deerfield Beach, FL 33442-8190

Cover design and chapter openers by Lisa Camp
Inside book design and formatting by Dawn Von Strolley Grove

*Half the world is composed of people
who have something to say but can't,
and the other half of people
who have nothing to say
and keep on saying it.*

Robert Frost

CONTENTS

ACKNOWLEDGMENTS

To Rabbi Noah Weinberg and Rebbetzin Dena Weinberg, for changing our lives and changing the course of history—not necessarily in that order.

To Kim Weiss of Simcha Press, for asking me to develop this project with Bob Burg, and for believing in my ability to make it happen.

To Bob Burg, for his invaluable input and for inspiring me with his desire to learn, grow and change, while helping others every step of the way—and for introducing me to Kim.

To Peter Friedmann and Allen Berg, for their generosity and support through the years.

To my parents, Joel and Phyllis Zelcer, for their constant belief in me. Special thanks to Mom for proofing the manuscript and giving valuable feedback.

To Genese Lieberman, Rob Sheinbein and Dr. Bob Schiermeyer, for the PC and laptop support. Without you there would be no technology, without technology there would be no book.

To David Lieberman, author and friend, for all of his guidance and encouragement.

To Rabbi Zelig Pliskin, for helping bring the awareness of guarding one's tongue to the world.

To Rabbi Yaakov Palatnik, Steve Eisenberg and Rabbi Mitch Mandel, for helping me "To the Source."

To my sweet kids who patiently put up with Ima writing another book.

To my husband, Rabbi Yaakov Palatnik, my keenest critic and my greatest fan.

To the women of Toronto, South Florida and Denver, who have faithfully attended my classes over the years and who continually inspire me to be more.

To the Almighty, for all the pain and all the pleasure.

Lori Palatnik

To Kim Weiss of Simcha Press, for being the wonderful, kind, encouraging person she is, for believing in this mission and suggesting that Rebbetzin Lori and I work together on this project.

To Rebbetzin Lori Palatnik, whose work I admired long before I even met her, for welcoming me to work with her on this project, and for touching so many lives in such a positive way. It's *her* wisdom being shared in this book. I'm really just adding some personal insights, but she'll never let you know that.

To Rabbi Zelig Pliskin, for carrying on the work of the Chofetz Chaim and teaching the world (including me) both the spiritual as well as personal dangers of *lashon hora* or gossip. Rabbi, you are a very sweet, humble man.

To Rabbi Moshe Goldberger, my "chavrusa" (personal teacher), for taking time to share so much of his wisdom over the past few years. Very few people are as loved by as many people as you are.

To Susan Tobias, editor extraordinaire. Thank you, Susan, for going above and beyond, and putting your heart and soul into making sure everything read exactly as it should.

To my parents, Mike and Myrna Burg, a shining example of how a marriage partnership between two wonderful people can provide a lifetime of joy and bring out the best life has to offer. I love you both so much that even the most elegant words could never provide an adequate description.

And, of course, to the Almighty for allowing me to be His servant. If I may paraphrase Dad, thank You for never letting me lose faith and confidence in You as You teach me, test me, discipline me, guide me, protect me, heal me, lead me on Your way, and make me part of Your game plan, for I know that everything You do is for Your sake. For on that day, You are One and Your Name is One.

Bob Burg

FOREWORD

Bob: Hi, I'm Bob, and I like to gossip.

Group: Hi, Bob.

Bob: Not only do I like to speak gossip, I like to listen to it as well.

Group: (all nodding heads in agreement and understanding).

Bob: In fact, not only do I like to speak gossip and listen to it, but I approve of it and encourage others to do the same. Yes, I am a gossip!

Group: (gives loud round of acknowledging applause).

If there were, in fact, an organization such as "Gossipers Anonymous," the above could very well have been true—and this would have happened to me not more than four or five years ago. Gossip was a very big part of my life. Yes, I was a nice guy. I just didn't realize the destructive capabilities of this awful habit (and it is a habit, as opposed to alcoholism, which is an actual disease). I also didn't realize to what level—whether measurably destructive or not—it was just plain wrong!

This habit of speaking badly about others, gossiping and repeating information that I had no right to repeat, attracted me throughout my childhood, and throughout my school years, even though my parents were very much against it and stressed how wrong it was. You'd think with such a great example it would not appeal to me, but it did. Later, my work environment—in the broadcasting business as a radio and television personality—put me smack dab in the middle of it as well. Then again, I suppose that's true of most of the workplaces throughout the world.

Upon leaving broadcasting and entering sales, it was much of the same. Then, however, I talked about my fellow salespeople and the awful prospects and customers with whom I had to interact. Finally, I became a speaker and author. You know what I found out? If you really want to speak and listen to this stuff (which I did), there are plenty of opportunities in this field as well. In other words, there was no one to blame but myself.

Fortunately, about four or five years ago I was reading a book, *Consulting the Wise,* by my now dear friend and teacher Rabbi Zelig Pliskin. In one particular chapter, he discussed a renowned sage who had dedicated his life to eradicating from the world the habit of gossip.

Feeling emotionally "hit between the eyes," I immediately became fascinated by this topic. I quickly ordered another book by Rabbi Pliskin entitled *Guard Your Tongue,* which took many of the laws of speech and boiled them down into easy-to-understand and simple-to-apply concepts. I was enchanted by the book and decided to make the breaking of gossip and hurtful speech my number-one personal self-improvement goal. I may not be all the way there, but I'm getting closer and closer all the time. I take special pleasure when people say such things to me as "Bob, I've known you for almost two years now, and I've never heard you say a bad word about anybody." I can't think of a much nicer compliment than that.

About a year ago, I was introduced to another special person and teacher in my life. Actually, I'd heard a lot about her previously, as she was already a very well-known author of books on Jewish wisdom. When I first heard that Lori Palatnik and her husband, the Torah scholar Rabbi Yaakov Palatnik, were at the same conference as I, I was anxious to find them and introduce myself. They were known to have a great partnership when it came to bringing formerly inactive Jewish communities together into cohesive units. This is accomplished through wisdom, hard work, continuous outreach and, mostly, a whole lot of acceptance and loving-kindness, which is what I've always believed is the mark of true leaders.

I was not disappointed. Their first offering after "Hello" was an invitation to their Friday night Sabbath table, as they had just moved to Florida within an hour's drive of me. How fortunate for me (though they've now moved to Denver)! Since then, I've gotten to know them both, as well as their incredible children. I believe you'll love meeting Lori in this book.

Getting back to the purpose of this book—simply put—it's to extinguish the fire of evil speech and help people to live in a gossip-free world, or at least a gossip-free environment (sometimes we must think globally but act locally, beginning with ourselves). The result? Positive interactions with the people around you, the healing of all relationships and, generally, a happier you.

Sound good? It is. And you can do it.

It takes effort to break a lifetime habit, as I am attempting to do, but the results are worth it. I look at the world in a completely different way now, and the world looks at me in a whole new light. All of my relationships, be they personal or business or even brief day-to-day encounters, have improved 1,000 percent.

If you have ever had a conflict with another person, there is a good chance it is based on the misuse of the gift of speech. Yes, it is a gift, and unfortunately we have taken it and used it for destruction. I am sure that wasn't the intention of the Creator of the World.

Throughout this book, you'll find references to the Biblical laws regarding speech and how they relate to our modern world. You'll also learn via real-life examples how to break the gossip habit and how to teach others to do the same. I truly believe that after reading this book, you'll know skills that will improve your life, help you get along better with others, and assist you in mending old hurts and reclaiming lost relationships. You'll also learn how to keep good relationships from going bad because of unnecessary words that hurt, and you will learn instead how to speak in a more encouraging, productive manner that strengthens those relationships you already have.

This book is for anyone who recognizes the possibility that gossip of any kind is destructive to their lives, the lives of those they love and the lives of anyone else with whom they come into contact. Personally, I welcome you to this journey, and congratulate you for choosing to become a part of it.

Bob Burg

PREFACE

I speak on many subjects throughout North America and abroad; my most popular talks are "Soul and the Afterlife," "How to Get Your Prayers Answered," and "The Ten Secrets to a Great Marriage." But by far, the talk that has the greatest and most immediate impact is the one on gossip. The titles vary: "True Lies," "Death by Gossip," "The Ten Pathways of Positive Speech," but the results are the same. People leave being completely sensitized to the pain and destruction that gossip can bring and resolved to eliminate it from their lives. People often tell me that after the talk they suddenly become acutely aware of how much time people spend talking about other people, most often in a negative way—and how much time they spend listening to it.

When people clean up their speech, they clean up their lives. Suddenly, a sense of control is embraced, self-respect is enhanced, and the respect of others is earned. Relationships heal, positive role modeling is in place, and peace is in the air.

After every talk I sell books that I have written, and everyone asks me, "Is there a book on tonight's talk—on gossip?" I always had to say "no," until now.

I met Bob Burg, an author and motivational speaker, when I lived in Florida, and he became a frequent guest in our home. He told me how learning about the laws of speech, founded in

Biblical tradition, changed his life. He introduced me to Kim Weiss at Simcha Press, and she asked us to get all of this down on paper so that other lives could be impacted for the good.

So here it is. Please read it and think about some of the ideas we have shared. Even if reading this book results in you stopping yourself *even once* from speaking badly about someone, Bob and I have succeeded. It's not all or nothing—every positive step counts. And if you gain something from this book, please pass it on to someone else. Let's make positive speech contagious. Let's change the world, one word at a time.

Lori Palatnik

The soul, like the body, lives by what it feeds on.
Josiah Gilbert Holland

Great minds discuss ideas.
Average minds discuss events.
Small minds discuss people.
Sign in a pizza shop, Miami Beach, Florida

1

Feathers in the Wind

Gossip is the art of saying nothing in a way that leaves practically nothing unsaid.

Walter Winchell

A nineteenth-century folktale tells about a man who went about slandering the town's wise man. One day, he went to the wise man's home and asked for forgiveness. The wise man, realizing that this man had not internalized the gravity of his transgressions, told him that he would forgive him on one condition: that he go home, take a feather pillow from his house, cut it up, scatter the feathers to the wind and return when done to the wise man's house.

Though puzzled by this strange request, the man was happy to be let off with so easy a penance. He quickly cut up the pillow, scattered the feathers and returned to the house.

"Am I now forgiven?" he asked.

"Just one more thing," the wise man said. "Go now and gather up all the feathers."

"But that's impossible. The wind has already scattered them."

"Precisely," he answered. "And it is as impossible to repair the damage done by your words as it is to recover the feathers. Your words are out there in the marketplace, spreading hate, even as we speak."

How interesting it is that we humans, so quick to believe the bad that others say about someone, so accepting of the "news" contained in print and television tabloids, and so ready to assume the worst regarding another's actions, actually allow ourselves to believe that the evil we spread about someone won't really matter. It's notable that *we* can't seem to immediately and resolutely accept the fact that the gossip we speak can do—and often does—significant damage to the subject of our chatter.

Paul Myers, a friend of Bob, says, "Gossip is like a fired bullet. Once you hear the sound, you can't take it back." That is what the nineteenth-century villager found out in a very disappointing, shameful moment of self-discovery. And it isn't just what we say *about* someone to others, but also what we say to that person directly. We've all been told "Sticks and stones may break my bones but names will never harm me," and we also know it is totally untrue. While a body will typically recover from a physical injury, the harm caused by direct insults can sometimes last a lifetime and tear the self-esteem right out of a person.

On the other hand, kind, encouraging words can build people's self-esteem, help them to grow and provide the impetus needed to do great, significant things with their lives. The choice regarding how we speak about or to someone is ours. It's called "free will."

2

Body and Soul

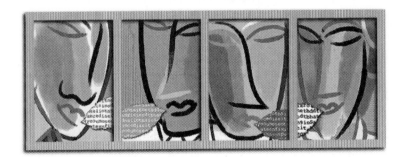

We are not physical beings having a spiritual experience, but spiritual beings having a physical experience.

Source Unknown

Mastering the gift of speech serves no purpose unless you realize that you are not just a body, but also a soul. If you believe you are simply a body, put down this book and do whatever you want, as long as you don't get caught. You can live the bumper sticker "Whoever dies with the most toys, wins." Living life only as a body infers there is no ultimate justice, no Higher Authority and no rules, except those imposed by humans.

If you know you have a soul given to you by a Creator, then living life is another matter entirely. It means that what you do really does matter, even if no one knows about it. It means there is ultimate justice. It means that the choices we make in this world make a difference, not just for here and now, but for eternity.

You do have a soul, and it is the essence of who you are. You are probably nodding in agreement, as I think almost everyone would. If I stood outside your local mall asking everyone who passed "Are you a body, or are you a body and a soul?" I think almost 100 percent would answer "I am a body *and* a soul."

Yes, we say it, but how many of us *live* it? How many of us wake up every day realizing that God has given us the gift of another day, that once again our soul has been restored?

I am married to a rabbi. But I don't wake up every day saying

"I'm a soul, I'm a soul!" No, I wake up bleary-eyed (hey, I've got five kids!), stagger to the bathroom, dress, wake my children, eat, drink, do a carpool, finish a chapter for my publisher, shop, eat again, drink again, go to the bathroom, do more carpools, feel hot, feel cold, feel tired. Hey, it's a very physical, body-oriented world. Even when married to a rabbi, you can forget that you are a soul.

Yet God has a way of reminding us. We all have had experiences when we know we are not just bodies but are souls. These are soul-awakening moments. Take a moment now and reflect. Think of a time in your life when you had a soul-awakening experience.

Perhaps it was the birth of a baby—a very physical experience, but certainly one that is soul-filled. A woman is a mini-creator, bringing forth life. At birth, a miracle is happening, and a new soul comes into this world. It's magic.

Have you ever gone into the countryside and looked into a night sky free from smog or city lights? You see thousands of stars, points of light that go on forever. You lift up your hand and you can almost touch eternity.

Ever have a near-death experience? Whoa—there's a wake-up call! I knew a man who accidentally fell from a third-story balcony. He lived to tell the tale, and his life was forever changed. Every year on the anniversary of the fall, he has a celebration and publicly gives thanks "for the best day of my life." He says that until that day he was living completely as a body, on the fast track of life, cultivating the proverbial "wine, women and song." He was the coolest, most popular guy in his social group, moving "up" just as fast as he could.

Then the fall stopped him in his tracks. When he was released in a wheelchair from the hospital and arrived home to recover, he phoned my husband and said, "Rabbi, I know that God saved me from this fall. Not only did I live, but the doctors say my recovery so far has been miraculous, and they expect me to walk again." Then he said something much more profound. "Yes, God saved me from this fall, but I also know that He pushed me, and I want to know why."

My husband spent time with him, and together they planned a different direction for his life.

Every year this man publicly gives thanks and says, "On that day, God did me a great kindness. He got my attention. Until then I was living as a body, and from that day on, I was awakened to the fact that I was also a soul."

The ultimate soul-awakening experience is witnessing death. The death of a loved one can awaken within us every emotion possible. Suddenly, the physical, mundane annoyances in life mean nothing. No one is standing at a graveside thinking, *Gosh, I forgot to take the chicken out of the freezer. What am I going to make for dinner?* Everyone is standing at a graveside thinking *What is life all about? What happens after we die? Is there a God? Am I living my life the way I should?*

September 11, 2001, was the ultimate modern-day, soul-awakening moment for the entire world. Thousands of people lost their lives, impacting their families and friends, as well as tens of millions of others. Countless people reexamined their lives. People made life decisions like never before. Reports chronicled a surge of people committing and recommitting to marriage. Many people shared with my husband and me their feelings that they realized that certain aspects of their lives until that point had lacked depth and meaning, and now they were going to turn them around.

People trapped on the doomed planes and in the World Trade Center buildings made last-minute calls to their families. No one spoke about selling his or her stocks or buying a new car. People said, "I love you," and "Take care of the children. I trust that you will raise them well."

We clung to one another that day, and the days that followed, reconnecting like never before, resolving to be better people. Family members who had previously been estranged made peace. Friends who had been feuding for years reached out to each other and put aside differences.

What happened? Tragic death and near death dramatically lifted us out of our everyday "body" lives and thrust us all into a state of "soul." We all asked, "What is life all about? What are we living for? Am I living my life the way I should?"

Yes, September 11 was a soul-awakening experience.

An interesting article appeared that week. It reported that the writers of gossip columns had stopped writing. They recognized that their columns were inappropriate in the wake of such an event. Who wanted to read gossip about celebrities at a time when people were focusing on creating a more meaningful existence? One columnist said that gossip was inappropriate now, *at least for a few days* (my emphasis). Even she recognized that what she did for a living had little value and would be scorned in the wake of the tragedy. However, people soon fell back into their old habits of getting pleasure from gossiping and talking negatively about other people's lives.

We are not just bodies, we are also souls, and every time we choose to speak badly about someone, we are harming our souls. If we stopped for even a split second to reflect on the appropriateness of what we are about to say and listen to our inner voice, there's a good chance we would decide not to speak.

The idea that you are harming your soul is a difficult concept to grasp. Because we are so physical, we have a hard time relating to something that we can't physically hold and touch. Yet consider this about love: You can't hold onto it—but it is as real as the fingers on our hands.

Scared Straight

To get smokers to stop smoking, a dramatic technique is used to scare them straight. Someone shows the smoker a picture of a pair of healthy lungs, and then a picture of the smoker's lungs. Smokers always know that with each puff they are damaging their lungs and harming their overall health, but because they can't see inside their bodies, their human tendency to rationalize blocks their ability to see the truth. If we could see a picture of our souls every time we gossiped, cheated, or lied, or made any wrong, selfish decision, we would see the effect it was having on our souls—and we'd all be scared straight.

Your soul is as real—or in a deeper sense, more real—than anything physical you can experience in this world. It is truly who you are. Your body is on loan, temporarily, a vessel to house the real you, which is your soul. One day you will give your body back. Only God knows how long you will have it.

Our souls, however, are eternal. They never die. Our life span in this world is minuscule compared to the scope of eternity. It is a world of opportunity, a world of choice.

Our souls' ultimate eternal pleasure will be based on the choices we make here. So choose wisely.

In the Bible, God says, "I have placed before you today the life and the good, and the death and the evil . . . choose life."[1] Does that mean you should choose to breathe? No, it means choose life—choose what is right, choose meaning, choose to strive—choose life.

Learning the laws of positive speech, given to us some thousands of years ago, will help sensitize and guide you to always choose what is right. It is not always the easy choice, or the socially acceptable choice, but it is the right choice. Have the courage to do it, and you will see all of your relationships transform, including the one with yourself.

> *The one thing in the world of value,*
> *is the active soul.*

Ralph Waldo Emerson

3

The Power of Speech:
A Gift Like No Other

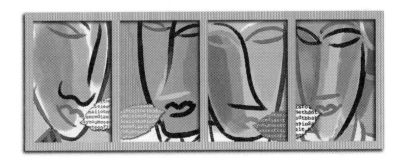

Speech is human nature itself,
with none of the artificiality of written language.

Alfred North Whitehead

The world itself was created through speech. In the Book of Genesis, each day of creation begins with the words "God said." On the first day, "God said, 'Let there be light.'"[2] On the second day, "God said, 'Let there be a firmament in the midst of the waters, and let it separate between water and water.'"[3] And every day after that, the narrative begins with "God said." The sixth day is where humans come in: "God said, 'Let us make man,'"[4] and this first person is described as "a speaking soul."[5]

Speech is where the body and soul meet—the soul's aspirations are given physical form and come into the world through speech.[6]

God has given humans the gift of speech, a means to communicate far beyond the capabilities of any other creation. While animals can convey messages and emotions in a limited way, only humans can share complex thoughts, intricate emotions and deep, philosophical ideas.

Have we done something significant with this precious gift? Have we used it for its ultimate good, letting a child know love, building self-esteem, moving groups toward positive goals, bringing people closer together, correcting an injustice? Or have we used it to destroy, malign, denigrate and separate people from one another?

Let's face it, gossip is one of the world's most destructive habits, and we're exposed to it practically everywhere we go and in much that we see—work, recreation, sports, home, in magazines, on television. There is absolutely nothing beneficial about gossip—it hurts *everyone* involved.

Marjorie and her sister, Amy, are no longer on speaking terms because their brother, Ken, told Marjorie that Amy told him that Marjorie had put on a few too many pounds due to her lack of self-control. Amy gossiped to Ken. Ken then gossiped to Marjorie. Not only are Marjorie and Amy not speaking to each other; they are also both mad at Ken.

Gossip hurts everyone. *Everyone!*

Tensions are high at the Ad Agency in Toronto. Lately, it seems almost as though alliances have developed—and not the type that lead to teamwork and increased production. These alliances are the result of people gossiping: talking behind each other's backs. Everyone is so worried they will be the group's next target that whenever they leave the room, they feel they need a "buddy system" just to survive from nine to five. Not that they trust their "buddies" either. By this time, the paranoia leaves no one completely trusting and no one completely trusted.

Gossip hurts everyone. *Everyone!*

David and Jerry used to be best friends. Then David told Jerry in front of some friends that he couldn't hang out with him that particular night because he had to do some home-work. That night, one of their friends saw David at the mall with a girl buying something. The friend reported the sighting to Jerry the next day, saying, "Hmm, so that's the homework he had to do." Jerry never gave David the opportunity to explain: The girl, his cousin, had called and begged him to pick her up because she didn't have a car and needed to get a gift quickly for their grandmother, who was sick in the hospital. After twice trying to explain to Jerry, David blew him off forever.

Gossip hurts everyone. *Everyone!*

CREATION SAYS IT ALL

If you stop and think about how God created everything with a purpose, and then you examine God's creation of the mouth, you may get some insight. He gave us a mouth that can open and can close, and He gave us a tongue surrounded by barriers—lips and teeth—all to teach us something: There are times to open our mouths, and there are times to close them, and there are times to put up barriers against what we are about to say.

The nature of an illness may also contain a message. When we become ill, we should stop and think what message it might hold for us. If the illness comes with laryngitis, we might ask if we are using the gift of speech properly. What can we learn from being sick in this way?

Speech is power.

Ralph Waldo Emerson

4

Consequences, Eternity and Other Scary Stuff

To get to heaven, turn right and keep straight.
Anonymous

Death and life are in the power of the tongue.
Proverbs 18:21

All right, brace yourself; here comes the really scary stuff. In chapter 2, we discussed the concepts of body and soul. We shared the idea that your soul is eternal and your body temporary. There is another world after this one, and the choices we make here make a difference to what happens there. (For more details see my book, *Remember My Soul.*)

However, certain actions can wipe out your eternity. One of them, arrogance, is discussed in chapter 11. In the Mishnah Torah, the great sage Maimonides says that an arrogant person has no place in Heaven. Arrogant people are so filled with themselves that there is no room for anyone else, and certainly no room for God. People who are masters of arrogance think that they are God.

Even more appropriate to what we have been discussing, the Mishnah Torah says that one who not only speaks badly about others occasionally but also lives and breathes it, that person has no share in the World to Come.

How appropriate! A person spends his or her whole life speaking badly of others, separating people from one another, and then God separates them from the rest of humanity for eternity.

Ready for another one?

It says in Kabbalah[7] that before you are born God assigns you a certain amount of words. Once you use them up, your life is over.

Be not rash with your mouth, and let not your heart be hasty to utter a word before God; for God is in heaven and you are on Earth, so let your words be few. For a dream comes from concern, and foolish talk from many words.

Ecclesiastes 5:1

So use your words wisely. Don't waste your allotment on being petty, vicious, judgmental and critical. Don't use those precious words to speak about other people's business, to gossip or to bring strife. "Say little, and do a lot."[8]

Every word is a gift. Open each one up and use it for good. Share words of encouragement, love, praise, depth and wisdom.

It's your choice. Choose life.

A man in the street exclaims, "Who wants to buy the elixir of life?" Everyone crowds around him, eager to buy. The man pulls out the book of Psalms and reads chapter 34:12–13, "Who is the man who yearns for life, who desires years of good fortune? Guard your tongue from speaking evil and your lips from deceitful speech."

Talmud

*Heaven will be inherited by every man
who has heaven in his soul.*

Henry Ward Beecher

5

Why Do We Gossip?

> *Gossip is always a personal confession,*
> *either of malice or imbecility.*
>
> Josiah Gilbert Holland

Evil speech can destroy friendships, break up marriages, and completely ruin businesses, neighborhoods, clubs, organizations, children, schools, religious institutions, boards, communities, partnerships, political parties—the list goes on and on. So why on Earth do we do it?

If you consider the reasons behind evil speech, you quickly realize that its source lies in very unhealthy rationalizations, which include the following:

1. If I put others down, somehow I will feel "up." The worse I paint the lives of others, the more my life looks better. *(Why do you think people watch soap operas? There is a psychological payoff to seeing people with messed-up lives. Somehow it gives us the illusion that our own lives aren't so bad.)*

2. When I gossip I am popular, and I get everyone's attention. All eyes are on me and now I feel like a "somebody" (but at someone else's expense). *(You may feel popular at the moment, but you are certainly not the person who others will come to trust and respect.)*

3. Life is boring—gossip makes it more interesting. *(Pretty sad if destroying other lives is how we overcome our own emptiness and make our lives more interesting.)*

4. What else is there to talk about? *(How about how we can*

help others, the meaning of life or ten ways to have a more loving marriage—among a thousand other positive topics?)

5. Because it is accepted. In fact, not only is it accepted, it is encouraged. Some journalists even fight hard to work up to the title of "gossip columnist." Certain television talk shows invite guests on weekly who are "gossip experts." *(This may be the most nonsensical title of all. What an awful area in which to be considered an expert.)*

If you do a search on the Internet for the word "gossip," as I did recently using the Google search engine, in ten seconds you will find links to approximately 1,520,000 sites.

You might ask, "But Rebbetzin Lori and Bob, no matter how hard I try to stop gossip even in my own little world, how can I be assured I will ever succeed?" Great question, and the answer will help you rest easily, while doing your part. As the wise Rabbi Tarfon said, "It is not your duty to finish the work, but you are not at liberty to neglect it."[9] In other words, do your best; it is up to God to see the mission completed in His time frame.

The reasons people speak destructively constitutes a long list, but clearly these reasons derive from a very bad place, a place of insecurity, self-absorption, pettiness, and further feelings of inadequacy.

A psychologist I know once pointed out that speaking badly about people is a form of projection. What you don't like about yourself, you tend to point out in others. Be aware of this, and soon what you personally need to work on will become clear.

In ending this section, I leave you with a quote from a noted scholar, Mrs. Tzipporah Heller, who says this: "There is no cheaper high for self-importance addicts than trivializing and belittling others. It gives such people the feeling of superiority without any need to actually be superior."

We speak little if not egged on by vanity.

François de La Rochefoucauld

6

The First Pathway: Speak No Evil— And Avoid Destroying Those Around You

*A cruel story runs on wheels, and every hand
oils the wheels as they run.*

Ouida

*Even in your thoughts do not curse a king,
and in your bedchamber do not curse the rich,
for a bird of the skies may carry the sound,
and some winged creature may betray the matter.*

Ecclesiastes 10:20

What goes around, comes around.

Anonymous

To the Source

What is more well-known than the burning bush scene in the Bible? Moses, a shepherd, is guiding his sheep in the wilderness, when suddenly he sees a bush on fire that is not being consumed.

God called out to him from amid the bush.[10]
And he said, "I am the God of your father, the God of Abraham, the God of Isaac, and the God of Jacob."[11]

God tells Moses that He has seen the affliction of the Jewish people as they are enslaved in Egypt. He tells him He will rescue them from oppression, and He commands Moses to go to Egypt to make it happen.

Moses replied to God, "Who am I that I should go to Pharaoh and that I should take the Children of Israel out of Egypt?" And He said, "For I shall be with you—and this is your sign that I have sent you: When you take the people out of Egypt, you will serve God on the mountain." [12]

Moses is still not convinced that he is the man for the job. He asks how to explain God to the Hebrews. God tries to reassure him:

Go and gather the elders of Israel and say to them, "The God of your forefathers has appeared to me. . . ." [13] *They will heed your voice."* [14]

Moses responded and said, "But they will not believe me and they will not heed my voice, for they will say, 'God did not appear to you.'"

God said further to him, "Bring your hand to your bosom," and he brought his hand to his bosom; then he withdrew it and behold, his hand was leprous like snow. He said, "Return your hand to your bosom," and he returned his hand to his bosom; then he removed it from his bosom and behold, it reverted to be like his flesh. [15]

This is not a magic trick; it is a confrontation with a huge lesson. Here you have Moses, meeting God for the first time, and God assures him that He will be with him and that the Hebrews will listen to him. Yet Moses continues to insist that they won't. Then you have the miracle of Moses putting his hand against his chest, his hand becoming leprous and then becoming fine again.

Moses had exceeded the bounds of humility in trying to refuse the assignment God was giving him. Moses crossed the line by beginning to speak evil about the Jewish people. *"But they will not believe me."* Not only was he not listening to God, but he had also lost faith in the Jewish people.

The punishment in the Bible for speaking badly about people is that those who gossip and speak evil will develop skin lesions similar to those of leprosy. This scourge will spread to their clothes and even to the walls of their homes.

This is a selective consequence that follows the principle "Measure for measure." When one speaks evil about a person, one encourages negative opinions about others, which causes people to separate from one another. The punishment from God, the leprosy, causes others to separate from the evil-sayer: Measure for measure. Even the sister of Moses was not immune to such disciplinary action: She was afflicted with *tzaraas,* a form of leprosy, and quarantined because she spoke badly about her brother.[16]

I clearly remember an incident in high school that relates to this matter:

Graduation was approaching. Awards were traditionally given to students at the end of the year for various accomplishments. Nominees for overall achievement awards—the most coveted of the honors—were put forth by the students and voted on by the faculty. Two awards were given, one for outstanding male student and one for outstanding female student.

One girl, who had accomplished much over her four years in high school, wanted the award very badly, and looking at her school record, both academic and extracurricular, it seemed she deserved it. She also had a male friend who was part of her inner social circle of high achievers, and she wanted him to win as well.

On the day of nominations, it leaked out that a certain guy from "the other crowd" was nominated as well, in direct competition to her friend. She loudly announced her displeasure, calling the other guy some very nasty names and mocking his nomination.

In the end, her male friend did win the award and, though she was nominated, she lost. The bitter outburst had been heard by a teacher, and it overrode four years of hard work. Even if the young woman deserved the award on paper, the faculty were looking for someone who deserved it in life.

There are laws based on Biblical tradition that govern how we use our speech. Those regarding their transgression are called the Laws of *Lashon Hora,* a Hebrew term that literally means "evil speech." These laws clearly outline when one is *forbidden* to speak about another, when one *is obligated* to speak about another and when one is allowed or forbidden to repeat information, as well as other laws that concern lies, gossip, slander and other such uses of speech. *Lashon hora* is considered one of the greatest of all Biblical transgressions and has created a world of conflict, strife and hatred.

Evil speech destroys lives. Following the laws carefully is the key to creating incredible peace, harmony and unity among people.

Your Children's Sports

If you have a child who plays Little League baseball, softball, youth soccer or any of the other sports that bring rooting parents to the stands, you've probably also witnessed some of the most horrific—not to mention mind-boggling—displays of damaging speech imaginable. And I don't mean from the children (although I'll address that in a moment) but from the parents! That's right—the parents. The words that come out of their mouths are despicable, insulting to the umpires and referees, the coaches, and even some of the other players.

The Jupiter-Tequesta Athletic Association in Jupiter, Florida, took such behavior in hand by insisting that all parents attend a "training" before being able to attend a game. The association also instituted rules regarding punishments for parents who became too outspoken during a game. Apparently, punishments ranged from being forbidden to attend a certain number of games to being disallowed from attending any at all.

It's amazing to me that these rules are even necessary. After all, what kind of message does this send to our children?

If parents yell at coaches from the stands, should they expect their children to respect their coaches and be able to learn from them?

If parents yell disparaging remarks at teammates or at the opposing team, should they expect their sons or daughters to learn and live loving-kindness toward others, including their own teammates?

Encouragement is the solution: Encourage everyone. You don't actually have to root for the other team, but you certainly have no excuse whatsoever for saying anything derogatory—ever. And when any of your child's teammates "goofs"—and they will—encourage them, cheer them on, let them know it's okay and that they'll "get 'em next time." And if they don't get 'em next time? So what! Let them know that's okay, too. What a difference you'll make in the lives of these young souls.

The coach should enforce a rule that there is to be absolutely no negative talk between teammates for any reason. If a player makes a mistake, kids also can say they'll "get 'em next time." Should someone make a mistake on the field and a teammate insult him or her for it, the latter should have to sit on the bench until they've learned that's not the proper way to speak to a teammate. If players encourage their teammates, they should be verbally rewarded.

Little League and other sports are intended not only to teach a child to win a game and improve his or her skills, but to be a good sport as well. That behavior begins with the people kids look to as examples—their coaches and their parents. Teaching a child that winning is everything, even if it means bad-mouthing others, is really teaching your child to lose.

Words Can Kill

Words are bullets, and used in the wrong way, they can kill, on a certain level, more than any gun.

The Bible contains hundreds of commandments, and yet under most circumstances, very few require you to give your life rather than transgress them.

If a crazy person comes up to a Jew alone on Yom Kippur—the Day of Atonement and a time of fasting—holds a gun to his or her head, and says, "Eat this bacon sandwich or I'll kill you," what does the law require one to do? *Eat the bacon sandwich!* You don't have to give your life for the laws of *kashrut.*[17]

One of the commandments directs us not to lie. If someone puts a gun at your back and tells you to lie or you will die, what should you do? *Lie!*

Imagine the following scenario (I have used contemporary names and situations in order to clarify the message): Curly is a crazy lunatic who jumps Larry in an alley and says, "Unless you kill Moe, I am going to kill you." According to the Talmud, the question is, can Larry kill Moe in self-defense? After all, if Larry doesn't kill Moe, he will himself die, and the Bible allows one to kill in self-defense.

Can Larry kill Moe? The answer is *no.* But what if Larry is the most righteous clergyman in the Western world and Moe is a known drug dealer? The answer is still *no.*

What if Larry is a cancer scientist on his way to announce the cure for cancer that will save millions of lives, and Moe is an escaped drug addict, passed out in the alley, track marks up and down his arm and probably dying any minute of an over-dose? The answer is still *no.*

No matter how positively I characterize Larry, and no matter how negatively I portray Moe, Larry is never allowed to kill Moe: *You don't know who is more precious in the eyes of God.*[18]

The cancer scientist may have had the ability to discover the cure for cancer ten years earlier, but because he was so enamored with his own honor, he didn't apply himself to his full potential. The drug addict may have been raised in a Mafia family in which he was expected to be a hit man. Perhaps he rejected the life of a murderer and, having no skills to earn a living, sank into a life of petty thievery and drugs.

We meet people in "chapter three" of their lives—we don't know what was written in chapters one and two, and we don't know what will happen in chapters four and five. Yet we are often quick to pass judgment in chapter three despite the fact that we are all humans living in the present, dwelling on the past and worrying about the future.

God, on the other hand, is not bound by time and thus sees the whole picture. He is able to see past, present and future in one glance. He knows where we came from, He knows where we are at and He knows where we are going. Because of this, only He can judge.

Thus, we cannot kill an innocent person, even to save our own lives.

"Thou shalt not murder" is a commandment you must give your life to uphold rather than transgress. Incredibly, speaking badly of others, according to the Talmud, is worse than murder. Although you don't have to give your life for it, when you mis-use the gift of speech, it bears a burden beyond the physical killing of one person.

Evil Speech Is a Triple Murder Threat

Each time one speaks badly of others, it is like killing three people.[19] Who is dying?

1. The person speaking

In whose eyes is this happening? On one level, the person speaking is being killed in the eyes of God. The Almighty has given that person the gift of speech, and he or she is using it to pit one person against another, to put others down and to speak of other people's private business.

On another level, he or she is being killed in the eyes of all those who are listening. When you have "the goods" on someone and say to a group of people, "Guess what? I heard the real story about so-and-so's marital breakup," what happens? Everyone leans in to hear the juicy gossip, and you become the center of attention. You are, in a sense, being crowned! You become the queen or king of this moment.

But it's just a moment. If you are known as the type of person eager to speak badly of others or quick to share "the dirt" at any given time, you will not be the person others come to for advice or with whom they entrust their lives. After all, if you are so quick to speak badly of others, everyone knows that soon they will be fodder for your social hobby.

When Bob was a television newscaster, he was also an avid speaker—as well as listener—of gossip. According to Bob, "When I was with certain people, it felt like we were best friends; as though it were the two of us against the world. But

I also knew that the same was true for whomever my 'friend' was with at the time. If they talked about others so viciously, what did that tell me would be said about me when I wasn't the 'best friend of the moment'?"

Interestingly enough, not only did most of Bob's coworkers not trust people like this, but they didn't like them either. Of course, that didn't stop anybody from listening to all the juicy gossip.

The truth is that at any moment you can be the popular one, but in the long run, you are lessened in everyone's eyes if you gossip. When you speak badly of others, it is like committing slow suicide.

Did you ever wonder why gossip is called "the low down" and "the dirt"? Let's face it, putting others down only brings us down.

Some time ago, someone in my evening class on ethics shared the following story with everyone in attendance:

> I was attending a ceremony at our house of worship and my sister-in-law walked in dressed very inappropriately! She was wearing a revealing top and I just couldn't believe it. I pointed this out to my husband and told him that his sister had done it again. When will she ever learn?
>
> But my husband did not respond. He just stood there and stared at me. It's maddening. He does it every time I speak about people. Don't you think he should say something to his sister, or perhaps I should?

I responded by saying, "First, do not say anything to your sister-in-law. She won't be able to hear it from you. If you have that type of relationship, chances are she won't be able to hear the weather report from you, let alone a comment about her choice of dress—as this can often be a challenging relationship.

"Second, when you speak negatively about others, who is being lessened in your husband's eyes?"

The woman didn't have to think long. "I am," she whispered.

"You've got a good guy there," I answered. "Don't just hang on to him. Learn from him."

2. The person you are speaking about

The person who is the topic of discussion at hand is obviously being killed. Such people are going about their business innocently, oblivious to the fact that you are speaking about them and affecting the way others view them. Irreparable damage can be done with every word, whether the information is true or not.

Like the wise man's "feathers in the wind" (chapter 1), a person's reputation—their good name—is certainly a major part of his or her joy of existence. Money can always be earned back fairly easily, but a reputation for honesty, integrity, and kindness, for being a loving husband, a good parent, a charitable and righteous person, while developed over years, can be wiped away instantly in a flash of evil speech. Depending upon the circumstances, it may be nearly impossible to restore it to its original level.

The Japanese have a term that describes very well what happens when a person's reputation is damaged: The person is said to have "lost face," as if they no longer exist.

3. The person listening

The Talmud says that the person who is damaged most of all is the one who is listening. Worse than gossiping is *listening* to gossip!

We all know deep down that, although almost everyone does it, speaking badly about people is plain wrong. The person you are slicing up is being harmed to no end. Yet, we wonder, why in the eyes of God is the passive listener the one who is doing the most harm?

The answer lies in the word *passive*. Of all three parties, the listener is the only one who has the ability to stop the evil speech in its tracks. The speaker has already made the decision to speak badly of others. The one being spoken about has no control over the situation. The listener is the only one who has the power to change the course of the conversation, which is why God puts the onus on the listener.

My son pointed out to me that reading gossip is even worse than listening to it! Sometimes, he said, we are in a situation in which someone will blurt out something negative about a person, and we have heard it before we have had a chance to block it. However, reading gives us time to decide whether or not this is something we want to know about. If an article is a juicy exposé on a person's life—exposing private details that are surely embarrassing and damaging to that person's reputation—why do we spend even one second of our lives reading it, other than for a momentary thrill or as a sick form of entertainment at someone's expense? There can be no excuse that we couldn't help hearing something that was suddenly blurted out. Clearly we would have made a conscious choice to "listen" to things we shouldn't.

Reputations are destroyed, marriages are ruined, partnerships are broken—there is no end. Are you beginning to understand why Bob and I are so emphatic about one of the world's favorite pastimes? (In the next chapter we offer some practical suggestions on how to avoid listening to evil speech.)

Keep in mind that these Biblical laws apply not only to talking about people, but also about organizations, groups of people and an individual you probably never expected—*you*. Yes, you are not allowed to speak badly about yourself! If you put yourself down, you are transgressing these laws. By doing so, in essence you are saying that God blew it. *God doesn't blow it.* He made you in His image, and God doesn't make junk. So forget the self-deprecating dialogue. You are unique. You are special. You have potential for greatness. Now use that potential for good.

Truth is not exciting enough to those
who depend on the characters and lives of their
neighbors for all their amusement.

George Bancroft

7

The Second Pathway: Hear No Evil— And Avoid Destroying Yourself

*The only time people dislike gossip
is when you gossip about them.*

Will Rogers

To the Source

After escaping the slavery of Egypt, the Jewish people met with many challenges in the desert. Wars were fought and won; miracles saved them time and time again. At last they came to the Promised Land. You would think they would be eager to enter, but they were not. Afraid of what was in store, they sent in one man from each of the twelve tribes to spy out the land. The result would have ramifications for all time:

They returned from spying out the Land at the end of the forty days. They went and came to Moses and to Aaron and to the entire assembly of the Children of Israel . . . and brought back the report to them and the entire assembly, and they showed them the fruit of the Land.[20]

They brought forth to Israel an evil report on the Land that they had spied out, saying, "The Land to which we have passed, to spy it out, is a land that devours its inhabitants! All the people that we saw in it were huge! . . . We were like grasshoppers in our eyes, and so we were in their eyes!"[21]

The entire assembly raised up and issued its voice; the people wept that night. All the children of Israel murmured against Moses and Aaron. . . . So they said to one another, "Let us appoint a leader and let us return to Egypt!"[22]

Although they knew that God wanted them to enter the Promised Land and that He had been with them through every challenge they had faced thus far, they still believed the evil report and were ready to rebel against Moses and go back to Egypt. The spies had their own agenda and fears of entering the Promised Land and taking responsibility. They looked for only the bad and embellished their interpretation to discourage the others.

The result? The Jewish people began to speak badly about Moses and his brother, Aaron. Then God granted their wish and refused to let them enter the Promised Land. They panicked, changed their minds and asked to enter. But it was too late. God made them wander in the desert for forty years until a whole generation that believed the evil report died off. Only then were those who were left finally allowed in.

This is the power of listening to evil speech. We have not changed that much in a few thousand years. The following really happened to a friend of mine:

Janis was looking for the right guy for years, and was finally fixed up with Kevin, a man who she thought might be "the one." They had gone out three or four times and things were moving in a positive direction. One day she was out shopping and ran into Linda, a young woman who she knew as a friend of a friend. They exchanged pleasantries, and then Linda mentioned that she knew Janis was dating Kevin and said, "Janis, I know it's none of my business (that should have tipped off Janis right there), *but I know Kevin and he is not for you." And with that, she parted.*

Janis was shaken, and the next few dates with Kevin did not go well. Janis couldn't help but put a negative spin on almost everything Kevin did and said. Kevin, who had thought things were going well, was now completely confused. Janis had seemed so open and nice, and now it seemed he was dating a prosecuting attorney. He found himself always having to defend himself. Eventually he just broke it off.

It wasn't until years later that Janis found out that Linda, who had offered her unsolicited advice, had once dated Kevin. Seems she was heartbroken when it didn't last.

The following story relates something that happened recently. See if it sounds familiar:

Jason and Susan had been married for a few years and had three young children. One day Jason came home and shared with his wife his desire to live in Israel. At first she was taken aback, but her love for her husband and her own love of Israel got the better of her, and she agreed to look into the possibility.

Jason began to do research and not only shared with his wife all the details and plans, but he also began to tell close friends what they were thinking of doing. Much to his surprise, several of them expressed their own desire to do the same. For many it was just a dream, but to Jason it was a dream that could become a reality.

In order to give each other strength, they formed a club. Once a month for two years they met and shared their plans and valuable information they had gathered on how to move to Israel and establish a life there. Through government offices and other support groups, a wealth of information and helpful hints were at their disposal.

Out of ten couples, eight ended up moving to Israel successfully. And what happened to the other two?

A family from their community who had moved to Israel two years before had just returned. Coming back was difficult, and they felt like failures. In order to justify their return, they played up all of the difficulties and troubles of living in Israel to anyone who would listen.

Two families listened and never went. Thankfully for Jason and Sarah, although they heard the talk, they decided to see for themselves. After a successful pilot trip, they took the plunge and have never looked back.

Of course they ran into challenges and cultural adjustments, but they say to this day that it is the best thing they ever did. Their positive experience was related weekly in e-mails sent out to the other families. Seven families followed them, all still living there happily.

Listening to evil speech is a choice. Choose wisely.

Moreover, pay no attention to everything men say, lest you hear your own servant disparaging you, for your own conscience knows that many times you yourself disparaged others.

Ecclesiastes 7:21–22

WHEN SOMEONE STARTS
SPEAKING BADLY ABOUT OTHERS

To avoid the self-destructiveness of listening to evil speech, one has to have concrete options for avoiding it. Following are some tried and true alternatives:

1. Keep walking.

If you are at a social gathering and you walk over to a group of people who you quickly realize are in the middle of a major gossip fest, keep walking! Don't put yourself into a situation where you will be forced to listen to gossip and slander.

2. Educate those involved.

Point out, in a kindly manner, that this is gossip and explain that it shouldn't be spoken about. This is the ideal response, as it educates the speaker and listeners to the fact that gossip is not right to do (everyone knows this on a certain level, but they do it anyway). However, this action often does not work and can backfire. If not handled properly, it could embarrass the person speaking (which is not your goal; embarrassing someone is like killing them[23]—and there's enough killing going on already), and it could backfire by turning the evil speech on you.

Educating those involved is a good method when you are in a one-on-one situation, where you can tactfully point out to the other person why evil speech is wrong.

3. Change the subject.

If a conversation starts to slide into a bad area, change the subject. Jump in with an exciting announcement regarding the local sports team, the weather, a cute story about one of your kids, a financial prediction—anything! Distract the speaker so that the flow of conversation is completely redirected into something that may be innocuous but safe.

There may be people in your life who have a greater tendency than most to speak badly about others. Perhaps you are related to them, or work at the desk beside them. If this is the case, when you are about to come into their realm, have a predetermined distraction story in mind, ready to be verbalized at any moment. That way, when you hear someone beginning to speak badly of others, you can jump in with "Hey, did I tell you the cute thing little Johnny said the other day? You're going to love this." Then you can launch immediately into a lengthy description of this child's latest antics. (Bring out the baby pictures if you really want to drive them away.)

That person probably can't wait until you take a breath so they can jump back in with their slanderous stories, so either don't breathe or, when they start up again, be ready to pull out another distraction. After awhile, it will be so difficult and frustrating for the speaker that he or she will give up and move on, hopefully understanding that gossiping in your presence has no payoff.

The key in stopping evil speech is the use of *tact*. Bob's dad defines tact as "the language of strength." Tact is a way of admonishing someone in such a way that not only do they not resent you for it, but they actually appreciate you for it. Easier said than done, but it can be done when you concentrate on protecting the person's ego while showing them.

For example, in helping "Diana" to see the destructiveness of speaking badly of others, begin by pointing out something positive about her: "Diana, I'm always glad when we can get together. You're such an interesting conversationalist." Then, give her an "I message"—a statement that briefly puts the onus of the challenge not onto her, which can cause defensiveness, but onto yourself, such as "This is just me, but I feel sort of uncomfortable talking about someone when they're not here." Finish with something positive, such as "You know about so many fascinating topics anyway, I'd rather discuss some of those. I'm always so impressed with your knowledge." (For more on the art of positive persuasion, see Bob's book *Winning Without Intimidation.*)

4. Judge the person being spoken about favorably.

Point out to the person speaking that there may be another side to the story. Remember the girl in our class we all thought was so stuck-up, and it turned out she was actually shy?

Offering a plausible explanation for the seemingly negative behavior of others may help diffuse destructive speech. If the boss grumbles when you walk by, don't start speaking badly about the grouchy boss. Think to yourself about the many reasons why this may have occurred. Perhaps someone in the family is ill and he is preoccupied with the situation. Perhaps he just received extremely bad news. Remember that you don't know what is really going on in anyone else's life.

Someone recently shared with Bob and me the following story:

I was waiting at the dentist's office. Time kept passing and still I wasn't being called in. I inquired with the receptionist, who told me that the dentist had not returned yet from lunch and that she expected he would arrive momentarily.

Others were in the waiting room, and one particular woman was incensed. "How dare he keep them waiting this long? Doesn't he have a cell phone? Why doesn't he call in? Call him!" The receptionist explained that she had tried to call but he wasn't answering his cell phone, and she tried to calm the woman. The woman berated the receptionist loudly and called the dentist every expletive imaginable, and eventually stormed out of the office.

The dentist never showed and the receptionist rescheduled all the patients present.

The next day the dentist was found dead in his garage. The police determined he had died the day before.

The person telling me the story was not only horrified at the death of her dentist, but she also told me that she couldn't imagine how the woman who previously felt so put-off now felt.

Give everybody the benefit of the doubt. In the end, only God knows who is right and who is wrong, and He will take care of everything. Your responsibility is to see the good, judge others favorably and avoid destructive speech at all costs.

5. "Zone out."

Were you ever in the middle of a conversation when you realized suddenly that your mind had wandered and you had no idea what the other person had been saying for the last few minutes? It's easy for us to "zone out" and think about a hundred things other than what is actually being said. You start worrying about what you are going to make for dinner, you suddenly remember a phone call you promised to return but didn't or you simply drift into dreamland.

That happens when you are *trying* to listen. The time to *let* your mind wander and drift is when someone starts speaking evil. Purposely zone out and go into a mental holding pattern so that the words are not registering. Do math equations in your head, compose a song, make a mental grocery list, count sheep—anything to avoid active listening. Try it—you can get very good at it.

6. Don't believe it.

If all else fails—you can't walk away (let's say you are the passenger in a moving car); you have tried to change the subject, but it keeps reverting back; you judged the person to the good, but to no avail; you tried going into a mental holding pattern but with little success—the only course of action is to *disbelieve* what is being said.

It is said that there are always three sides to any conflict— his side, her side, and the truth—and that *is* the truth. Even if the speaker sounds like he or she has all the facts right and claims to have a first-person account of all events, your obligation is to not believe what is being said.

Repeat in your head "I do not believe this. I do not believe this." It's difficult, very difficult, but if all else fails, this is your last resort.

Do you know those Perry Mason–type shows that feature a heated trial? The classic scene is when the prosecuting lawyer instructs a witness to blurt out something on the stand that is not allowed to be said—perhaps something incriminating from the defendant's past. The witness does as he is told, and the lawyer for the defense immediately stands up and yells, "I object!" The judge of course says, "Sustained," and then, "Those words will be stricken from the record," followed by "The jury will disregard what the witness just said."

Yeah, right. We all know the witness and his lawyer are smiling smugly to themselves, knowing that though officially stricken from the record, those words will never disappear. They are forever imbedded in the hearts and minds of every juror.

Not believing what we have heard is the hardest option of all. Yet we are forbidden to believe even one word of destructive speech that we hear, even if it sounds 100 percent true.

The following actually happened to me:

> Someone came running up to me before services and blurted out a piece of slander regarding a fellow congregant. I didn't have time to stop them or to use any of the tools of distraction or zoning out or anything. It was already said. My only option was to not believe what had just been told me. "I don't believe it. I don't believe it," I kept repeating to myself. "There is another side. There is another side." I really meant it. What was said likely could have been completely wrong. There were a million plausible explanations for what this person interpreted as evil.

> Every time I see the person who was slandered, even years later, the slander I heard immediately pops into my head. I have tried everything I can to erase it, to no avail. That incident really taught me the power of words. Once they are said, and you hear them, it's done.

Someone who attends one of my classes told me the following story:

> After hearing your lecture on positive speech I became very sensitized to the fact that most people spend most of their time speaking about others, almost always in a derogatory way.
>
> I was attending a religious service, and a man I know was in the pew in front of me. He turned around and started speaking badly about someone I know. I told him directly and firmly that I didn't want to hear it. He just kept talking. Again I repeated, "I do not want to hear this," but nothing would stop him.
>
> I realized that if someone has made the decision to speak badly, sometimes even a bulldozer won't stop them.

A recent guest at my family's Sabbath table confirmed this observation with her own story:

> I have been studying the Biblical laws of speech, but they are so difficult to uphold. Almost every day someone will insist on speaking badly about other people to me. They'll say, "I heard what happened to so-and-so, he—."
>
> I'll interrupt and say, "I don't want to know."
>
> "But don't you want to know what happened when he—?"
>
> "No," I say emphatically. "I don't." And then that person will proceed to tell me anyway!

Most people have ears, but few have good judgment.

Lord Chesterfield

8

The Third Pathway: Don't Rationalize Your Life Away

*Don't draw another's bow; don't ride another's
horse; don't mind another's business.*

Proverb

To the Source

We learn many things in the Book of Genesis, including
what can happen when someone decides to speak
badly about others. In one famous case, it happens
between brothers.

Jacob, one of the biblical patriarchs, settles in the land of
Canaan, along with his family, including his twelve sons (later to
head the twelve tribes of Israel). One of his sons is Joseph. He
would face many hardships and challenges in the years to come,
and it all begins like this:

> *Joseph, at the age of seventeen years, was a shepherd with
> his brothers by the flock . . . and Joseph would bring evil
> reports about them to his father.*[24]

Joseph thinks his intentions are good, rationalizing that his
brothers are making mistakes and it is his duty to tell his father.
However, he actually jumps to conclusions and misjudges them. He
could have related the facts to his father Jacob and let his father, in
his wisdom, decide what to do, but instead he offers a negative
interpretation that demeans his brothers in their father's eyes.

As if that isn't enough, it is clear that Joseph is favored by his father:

Now Jacob loved Joseph more than all of his sons, as he was a child of his old age, and he made him a fine woolen tunic (the "Technicolor Dreamcoat"). His brothers saw that it was he whom their father loved most of all, so they hated him; and they could not speak to him peaceably.[25]

This clear favoritism does not help matters. Joseph's negative reports, combined with sibling rivalry as the sons vie for their father's love and approval, results in continual misjudgment on everyone's part and increases to the point where the brothers turn on Joseph. At first they think of killing him, but instead they throw him into a pit and sell him as a slave, and he is eventually taken by force to Egypt.

This occurred thousands of years ago, and we still have not learned our lessons.

I want to share the following sad history of a more contemporary family:

A family of immigrants came to Boston and set down roots, starting from scratch in a new land. They had five children, three boys and two girls, who were raised to achieve their potential. Unfortunately, the message their father and society had given them was that potential meant material success above all else, so three of the brothers moved to Philadelphia to achieve just that. One went into the world of academia, but two threw themselves into real estate development, buying and selling land like there was no tomorrow. At first they invested in things together, but eventually one started dabbling in some independent projects, and soon they were both doing their own thing.

At first they celebrated each other's successes, but their competitive natures and their desires for their father's approval soon got the best of them. Secret deals were made in the city, with each brother trying to outdo the other. Both became very wealthy, very fast. Each one showered the father with gifts and trips.

Before long, their competitive drive led the brothers to incredible rivalry, with one eventually not speaking to the other, forcing friends and colleagues to take sides.

The brother who chose the world of academia was at first happy with his choice, but he clearly saw his brothers getting all the wealth and glory. He also saw what he felt were improprieties in their business dealings. He rationalized that he should go to his father and tell him what was going on between the two brothers, that the desire of each for success over the other had caused both to engage in illegal acts and was causing hatred between them. Perhaps, he thought, the father could straighten them out and make peace. In fact, though their business dealings had been maverick, they actually had done nothing illegal.

The father, who possessed a very strong sense of right and wrong, was devastated, refused any more gifts from his two bickering sons, and cut both out of his life. The third son felt his actions had made the situation spin out of control, but he also felt at a loss to make it right.

Eventually, the two brothers in business made peace with one another, but they never spoke to the third brother again.

The father died with some wealthy sons, but a shambles of a family.

I imagine that while reading this book you have agreed that some gossip is wrong, but you have also probably rationalized that sometimes it is not that big a deal. C'mon, you might say, let's not be so picky about every little word—what's wrong with a little juicy gossip between friends?

You are not alone. We all try to downplay the power of words and justify why we may use them any way we see fit, but no amount of creative rationalization can justify speaking badly about others. Following are some of the classic reasons why people rationalize they can do so:

1. "But everyone does it."

There isn't much to be seen in a little town. But what you hear makes up for it.

Kin Hubbard

Just because everyone does it, doesn't make it right. Remember how you gave this reason to your mother when you were young and wanted to do something she opposed? Remember what she said? (All mothers went to the same school of motherhood and are taught to say the same thing.) *"If everyone jumped off a cliff, would you do that, too?"*

Here's the rub to the rationalization that everyone does it: Not everyone does! That's right. Not everyone speaks badly about others. Some people not only don't gossip, but they continually abide by the well-known saying "If you don't have something nice to say about someone, don't say anything at all."

Typically (yet far from ironically), these people tend to be very popular and trusted. And why not? In a world in which many people gossip constantly, these people are the rocks, the good-hearted, trustworthy folks who simply refuse to go along with everybody, which, in essence, means there actually is *no* "everybody." The truth is that speaking badly is a personal choice.

Imagine a group of office workers hanging out by the water-cooler, making comments about fellow workers who are not there. (Not hard to imagine, is it?) The talk is that Jane has put on weight, Harry is messing up again and Steve is out of style.

Transform that scene to the school yard. Everyone is about ten years old. All the kids are there, and Jane is told she is fat, Harry is called a loser and Steve is taunted as a nerd—all to their faces.

It's not so pretty in the school yard, yet somehow we justify that it's okay to talk behind people's backs when we are older and more "mature."

2. "But it's true!"

*A truth that's told with bad intent
beats all the lies you can invent.*

William Blake

Actually, the classic definition of *lashon hora,* evil speech, is saying something that is true and reflects badly on a person. If something is not true, it falls under other laws of speech, but it is still forbidden to say it. When it comes to evil speech, truth is no excuse; it *is* the prohibition.

Let's take this a step further and ask ourselves "So what if it is true?" Why should that mean it is our job to spread a negative truth? If it can't possibly help anyone involved, but could possibly hurt those involved, why should we be spreading such a truth?

You and I may not think there is anything wrong, but the laws of speech say otherwise. And who crowned any of us the messenger of all gossip? Let's take off that crown; it is not becoming.

Who is the gossipmonger? One who carries reports and goes from one person to another saying, "So-and-so said this! And I heard such-and-such from this person!" Even if what he says is true, he destroys the world.

Maimonides[26]

3. "Everyone knows about it."

That which is everybody's business is nobody's business.

Izaak Walton

Even if it was on the front page of every newspaper, it would still be forbidden.

Case histories have been cited of lives that were ruined, of innocent people having been accused of crimes, pictures of them and hearsay splattered over the front pages, shaming them and their families. In the end, when the accused were proven not guilty of all charges, the articles sharing such news were buried in the back pages. The damage had been done, and no amount of exoneration could ever put together their shattered lives. Many people think where there is smoke there is fire, and even when someone is found innocent, doubt remains in people's minds.

It is said that there are three crowns to a person: the crown of wisdom, the crown of kindness, and the crown of holiness, but the greatest crown of all is the crown of a good name.[27] When you take that away, you take away a person's reputation now and for generations to come.

4. "If he were here, I would say it to his face."

Maybe you would, and maybe you wouldn't. But even when the person is standing right in front of you, that is not an excuse to speak in a destructive manner.

5. "Of course I am allowed to tell my spouse anything."

Marriage is our last chance to grow up.

Joseph Barth

The laws of speech also apply between a husband and a wife. If you think about it, of all the relationships we have, this is the most precious, the most sacred. Why would we want to blemish it with such talk?

I gave a talk in Denver on the subject of ethical speech. Two weeks later a woman came up to me at an event and told me she had been there at the talk. She shared the following:

Everything you said about how we speak badly of others made so much sense, but when you got to the part about not gossiping even to your spouse, well, that one bothered me. Can't I say anything to my husband? But then I thought about it, and what you said was right. How can I honestly say that gossiping to people is wrong, yet it is right when it is my own husband? I just got married a few months ago, and I went home after the talk and told my husband what you said. We made a pact then and there that our marriage was going to be based on something of value, on a higher plane than any other relationship. We made our marriage "gossip-free," and if one of us starts slipping, the other one is there to give the reminder. The positive energy this has created is truly amazing.

6. "I was only joking."

Humor tells you where the trouble is.

Louise Bernikow

In every joke there is an element of truth. Jokes can hurt, too. And this is often what we quickly use to justify saying something that wasn't really a joke at all, just another poor use of speech.

One of Bob's friends used to talk to and about people, making little insulting digs and then explain that he was "just kidding." Finally, Bob tactfully pointed out that if you have to follow up such comments by explaining that you were only kidding, it probably wasn't too funny in the first place and would have been better left unsaid. As the sages say, "Silence is the fence around wisdom."[28]

Bob's friend, Laura, had just begun studying the concept of not speaking badly of others and learning about the laws prohibiting gossip. She phoned to tell him about a friend of hers (who, of course, she did not name) who she had already helped begin to break the habit of evil speech. (One of the advantages of your friends knowing you are writing a book on this topic is that you get to hear lots of great success stories.)

Laura had been going on walks with her friend for about a year. Although very nice and well-meaning, the woman constantly spoke badly about others, from the beginning of any walk until the very end. Not surprisingly, she was constantly in the midst of feuds and arguments with different people for various lengths of time. Of course, it was always "their" fault—never hers.

Soon after Laura began learning about these laws, she gently began explaining them to her walking mate. As you may guess, it had little effect. This person kept speaking badly, and Laura, not sure what to do, kept feeling obligated to listen. Realizing that something had to be done—as listening to such speech is even worse than speaking it—she finally said, "Dolores (not her real name), tell me what's happening with you." Dolores responded, "What do you mean, what's happening with me?"

Laura replied, "Something must be happening in your life if you continue to speak so ill of these people. We don't talk about things like this unless there's something going on inside of ourselves that triggers it. I want to know what's going on inside of you that's giving you such bitter feelings about others, and keeps you gossiping about them."

According to Laura, this took Dolores by surprise (remember, most people encourage gossip, they don't try and stop it). At first, Dolores denied she had a problem. Laura let it drop but told her politely that to be able to keep walking together, she didn't want to ever again hear such talk.

Laura says, "I told her that if I could help her with a problem she was having with herself I'd be glad to, but that it could not include any destructive speech." Amazingly, reports Laura, Dolores approached her the very next day and told her she was right, that she has a lot of bitter and unresolved feelings within herself. She feels victimized by everyone, which stems from a lot of personal issues she has not yet worked out. She told Laura that she appreciated being able to walk and talk with her and that, from now on, destructive words would be left out of the conversation.

A friend of mine shared the following story:

I was newly engaged and meeting some of my future husband's relatives for the first time. My mother and sister accompanied me to the visit. The relatives turned out to be very eccentric and did and said a lot of strange things.

After spending the evening with them, we said our goodbyes and piled into the car with my fiancé driving. For the first ten minutes we drove in absolute silence. My mother was the first to speak. "Gee," she said, "this not speaking bad about people is really hard." We all broke out laughing. I guess just saying it was transgressing the laws, but it was still a much higher level than what could have transpired.

9

The Fourth Pathway: See No Evil—How Judging People Favorably Will Change Your Life

*Hesitancy in judgment is the
only true mark of a thinker.*

Dagobert D. Runes

To the Source

The story in the Book of Genesis concerning Joseph and his brothers is a long and meaningful tale that has important lessons for our lives today, including how misjudging others can lead to tragic consequences.

After Joseph is sold as a slave (see chapter 8), he is brought to Egypt, and many years later a famine comes to the land of Israel, forcing the brothers to leave and look elsewhere for food. Their search leads them to Egypt, not knowing that Joseph is living there.

Through hard work and divine help, Joseph has risen out of slavery in Egypt to become second in command to Pharaoh, overseeing the distribution of food to the people of the land.

Knowing of the famine in Israel, Joseph waits for his brothers to appear. When they do, they do not recognize him. Joseph then sets up a series of events to bring his brothers to the realization that they had wronged him so many years ago. They never really come to understand that or to truly repent, and Joseph eventually reveals himself to them. He tells them that Divine Providence sent him ahead to Egypt to be able to provide for his family in Israel, and he proceeds to take care of his brothers and sends for his father.

You would think the brothers would repent at this point and see from the beginning, and now, that Joseph only wanted what was best for them. Yet this is not what happens after Jacob arrives in Egypt and before he dies.

> *Joseph's brothers perceived that their father was dead, and they said, "Perhaps Joseph will nurse hatred against us and then he will surely repay us all the evil that we did him." So they instructed that Joseph be told, "Your father gave orders before his death saying, 'Thus shall you say to Joseph: O please, kindly forgive the spiteful deed of your brothers and their sin for they have done you evil'; so now, please forgive the spiteful deed of the servants of your father's God." And Joseph wept when they spoke to him.[29]*

Joseph wept because the brothers never understood his intentions. All he had wanted was for them to come to the understanding that they had misjudged him and for them to change their ways, but all they cared about was that he might take revenge against them. In a way they were admitting they were wrong, but then they repeated their mistake, misjudging Joseph again. Joseph's tears at this point are for his brothers, but in a deeper way he is crying because he knows that this character flaw of misjudgment is not to be corrected in his day and will haunt humanity in the future.

Even the prophets fell fate to misjudgment. In the first Book of Samuel, Hannah, wife of Elkanah, was so distraught after years of being barren, that she came to the Holy Sanctuary to beg God's mercy and blessing:

She was feeling bitter, and she prayed to God, weeping continuously. She made a vow and said, "God, Master of legions, if You take note of the suffering of Your maidservant, and You remember me, and do not forget Your maidservant, and give Your maidservant male offspring, then I shall give him to God all the days of his life. . . .

It happened as she continued to pray before God that Eli (the prophet and High Priest) *observed her mouth. Hannah was speaking to her heart—only her lips moved, but her voice was not heard—so Eli thought she was drunk. Eli said to her, "How long will you be drunk? Remove your wine from yourself!" Hannah answered and said, "No, my lord, I am a woman of aggrieved spirit. I have drunk neither wine nor strong drink, and I have poured out my soul before God. Do not deem your maidservant to be a base woman—for it is out of much grievance and anger that I have spoken until now." Eli then answered, "Go in peace. The God of Israel will grant the request you have made of Him."* [30]

This event had a happy ending, as Hannah did become pregnant.

She named him Samuel, for (she said) "I requested him from God." [31]

And Samuel became a great leader and prophet.

The tendency to quickly misjudge others permeates our lives today. How often have we accused someone, sometimes those we love the most, of wronging us or behaving in an improper way, only to find out that they hadn't done so at all?

A friend of mine told me the following story:

The tenants had gotten together to provide for the upkeep of the building where I live in a small condominium. We all agreed to share certain expenses, but in order to save money, we also rotated certain responsibilities. One of them was the weekly cleaning of the stairs and hallways, which were tiled. I was going away on vacation and checked to make sure that it was not my week to take care of the cleaning. In fact, it was the week that my downstairs neighbor always had her teenage sons do it.

I arrived back from vacation very early one morning, about an hour before anyone would normally start their day. As soon as I walked into the lobby, I was livid to see small puddles of water everywhere. My neighbor and her irresponsible sons had obviously done a very poor job of maintaining the common area. The further I entered the building, the more water I saw. Clearly they had just thrown down some water and half-heartedly mopped it up. Why, this was so dangerous! Someone could easily slip and fall.

I got into the elevator and as it rose I was thinking that I should just go straight to their door, wake them up, confront them with their negligence and demand that they mop up immediately.

As I got out onto my floor, I couldn't believe how much water I saw. This was not normal, how could—? Just then I saw what the real source of the negligence was. As I opened the door to my home, I could hear the running water. When I departed on my trip, I had left a tap dripping ever so slightly in a sink that was plugged. It had taken many days, but obviously during the last night it had turned into a flood throughout the building.

The only thing I was thankful for was not going with my first inclination and pounding on my neighbor's door. Can you imagine? It was a big lesson for me in judging people favorably.

The key to controlling destructive speech is to develop the ability to judge people to the good. Though touched upon in the previous chapter, this concept deserves a much more thorough examination because evil speech truly can be beat if we can perfect this action.

Remember how we spoke about meeting people in "chapter three" of their lives? We have no idea what went on in chapters one and two, and we certainly don't know what lies ahead in chapters four, five and six. Yet, even with this limited perspective, we are quick to judge. A person who seems at a low point may in fact have worked very hard to overcome hardship and reach even *this* level. Others, although they may look righteous and accomplished, may be using only a tiny portion of their talents and skills.

A lot of this stems from the educational system in which we were all raised. Tests and grades are used to evaluate students not on individual merit but in comparison to others. One student struggles in math, failing most semesters, but finally applies himself 200 percent and manages to eke out a C at the end of the term. Another student, naturally gifted in math, never cracks a book, yet scores an A–. On paper and in posted grades, the second student is head and shoulders above the first, but in the scheme of life it is the student who worked hard and truly achieved his potential who should be praised. The one with the A– had A+ potential, but he never really tried to achieve it.

It would be funny if someone praised you for how well you spoke English if you were born in the United States and have been speaking it your whole life! Yet sometimes we, and society, take pride in things we did nothing to deserve. In the world of truth, when we apply ourselves and work hard, we do have something to be proud of.

We can't judge another person *unless we have arrived at their place*.[32] It follows that since we can never be in exactly the same place and life circumstance as another person,[33] we are never allowed to judge anyone.

However, this shouldn't mean we are so open-minded we accept anyone and anything and any action. (My husband likes to say, "Don't be so open-minded that your brains fall out.") We can't judge a person, but we can judge actions. Yet even when people make mistakes, we can still see the best in them. We are commanded to love them and care for them in spite of their mistakes.[34] We see this with our children. Who knows their flaws better than we do? Yet we choose to love them.

Only God can truly judge a person, and His judgment is unique to the individual, not based on a formula. Maimonides pointed out that a person may achieve one merit that could outweigh a lifetime of mistakes.[35]

What is it about human beings that makes us assume the worst? "How could he not have returned my call?" "Why did she say that about me?" "I can't believe he'd bounce a check—what a crook!" "That cabbie definitely overcharged me—I was ripped off." "How irresponsible she is to have forgotten our appointment." Have any of those words ever left your lips (or sat angrily in your mind)? Most of us would have to admit the answer is yes.*

An excellent book on this topic is *The Other Side of the Story: Giving People the Benefit of the Doubt* by Yehudis Samet. It deals exclusively with finding a way to judge others favorably when it clearly "appears" they have wronged us. We highly recommend her book for an in-depth study of this topic. Like gossip, Bob considers this to be another area of his life he's had to work hard to overcome, and still does. In fact, most of us do, and for very logical reasons.

Humans tend to make decisions (both minor and major) based on very limited information, and through our own personal belief systems. Also, if something has happened before, it's easy to assume that similar circumstances will *always* lead to the same results, every single time. In fact, they don't. We are also "gifted" with "tunnel vision," seeing what we want to see. On top of that, human beings tend to be extremely self-absorbed.

For now, here's one proof regarding how we can know that not everyone appearing to have wronged us has actually done so.

You and I, at one time or another, have also been accused of doing something hurtful, inconsiderate or otherwise inappropriate

---

*By the way, here are some possible answers to that question from an earlier paragraph in this section: "He did return your call, twice, but your answering machine was broken." "She didn't say that about you—her remark was taken out of context by a 'friend' who just happened to overhear that part of the conversation." "He had just closed that account and didn't realize you still had not cashed his check" (an error on his part, yes, but hardly crooked). "The cabbie didn't overcharge you—the previous one had inadvertently undercharged you for the same distance, or possibly this time there was a required surcharge you weren't aware of." "She didn't forget your appointment. You forgot you were supposed to call first to confirm." I'm sure you can come up with more examples based on your unique personal experiences.

when, in fact, we didn't. At the very least, the person spreading such untruths could not have known about any extenuating circumstances at play. Isn't it an awful feeling to be misjudged or wrongly accused? To know a person might be harboring negative feelings toward us for something we didn't actually do, although it certainly did "appear" that way?

Your good friends, Mary and Tom, are outraged that you didn't invite them to the barbecue you held recently at your home. Worse, they found out about it the following week from another couple you did invite . . . whom you don't know nearly as well! Mary and Tom wonder what they ever did to you to deserve that "snubbing." Too hurt and disgusted to ask you, they carry a grudge until, two weeks later, you call them to apologize . . . because the invitation you mailed to them came back postage due. Yes, they feel terrible for having doubted your friendship. But, here's the kicker: For the past three weeks, you've been mad at them! Why? Because not only had they not accepted your invitation to attend your barbecue, but they didn't even have the courtesy to RSVP as you requested of those you invited!

Judging others favorably is always a good idea. It allows us to see the best in others, and to avoid very unnecessary negative feelings as well.

When the Bible says, "Love your neighbor like yourself,"[36] it means that you should treat others the way you want to be treated, and judge others the way you want to be judged.

Imagine being on your way to meet a friend and getting caught in an unexpected traffic jam; imagine that one of you is not carrying a phone and there is no way to reach your friend to tell her of the delay. Wouldn't you hope you would arrive and be greeted by a relieved and loving face? She was worried something had happened to you, perhaps a traffic accident. Or upon arrival you could find a fuming and offended ex-friend. How dare you keep her waiting!? How inconsiderate! Yes, you hope the person waiting for you judges you to the good. So, the next time you are the one waiting, instead of assuming you were carelessly stood up, assume that the person had good intentions but something unforeseeable came up.

Can you imagine a world where people really did this? It would be a beautiful world indeed.

I learned early in life not to judge others harshly. We outcasts are very happy and content to leave that job to our social superiors.

Ethel Waters

"But I Know a Person Who Is So Bad—"

Whenever I speak on this subject, someone always asks me how to deal with someone who is so evil that it makes his or her life a living hell. How can one possibly judge that person to the good?

Rabbi Noah Weinberg, my personal rabbi, knows the best response:

Rabbi Weinberg was lecturing to a group of thirty-somethings in Toronto. After speaking about judging people to the good, a woman put up her hand. "Rabbi, the ideas you shared are very nice, but you don't have my sister-in-law in your life.

"Every time I leave the room she stabs me in the back. She never has a nice thing to say about anyone. How can I possibly deal with her?"

Rabbi Weinberg answered, "Imagine you were at a corner ready to cross at a light. All of a sudden from behind someone shoves you into the street. You fall on your face and get up scratched and dirty; you turn, ready to give the person who shoved you some of the angriest words that you know. When you turn around and are ready to pounce, you see that the person behind you is wearing dark glasses and holding a white cane. How do you feel now? Instantly you calm down, and your anger turns to pity. He couldn't help it. He's blind.

"That," Rabbi Weinberg continued, "is your sister-in-law. She's blind. She doesn't wake up in the morning and decide to hurt people that day. She literally doesn't know what she is doing. She's blind. Instead of anger, have pity."

Rabbi Weinberg concluded by giving everyone a tool. "The next time your parent, in-law, coworker or neighbor does something to make you crazy, picture them wearing dark glasses and holding a white cane. They are blind. They can't see that they are doing wrong. Help them, guide them and show them gently the error of their ways. But don't expect them to change. A blind person can't see overnight. It takes time, and sometimes they will never see. Feel sorry for them."

Yes, it's hard to judge others favorably when it is so clear that they are completely in the wrong. However, if you can internalize the reality of the next statement, perhaps you can find it within yourself to judge even those people to the good:

> *God judges you the way you judge others.*
>
> Babylonian Talmud (Shabbat 127b)

If we want to be exacting in our judgment of others, to stand on pride, to focus on mistakes and lack of character, that is how God will judge us. If we strive to give the benefit of the doubt, to give people a second chance, to understand their circumstances, to be forgiving, God will do the same for us.

Which would *you* rather have?

> *It is well, when judging a friend, to remember that he is judging you with the same godlike and superior impartiality.*
>
> Arnold Bennett

10

The Fifth Pathway: Beware of Speaking Evil Without Saying an Evil Word

No one gossips about other people's secret virtues.

Bertrand Russell

To the Source

Although we are working at not speaking badly about people and not listening to gossip and the like, we must address the issue of how we can still transgress without technically saying a word.

In the Book of Genesis, Jacob travels to Charan to seek a wife from his mother's family. He is specifically looking for Laban, his uncle. He chances upon a well where shepherds are watering their flock.

> Jacob said to them, "My brothers, where are you from?" And they said, "We are from Charan." He said to them, "Do you know Laban, the son of Nahor?" And they said, "We know." Then he said to them, "Is it well with him?" They answered, "It is well." [37]

Here we get our first indication that Uncle Laban is not a very nice guy. Just look at the curt way the shepherds answer Jacob's inquiry. If someone came up to you and asked if you knew so-and-so and you answered succinctly, "I know," I think the person would get the distinct impression that you are not a big fan of the guy.

In the laws of speech, it's not just what you say but how you say it, and even what you don't say.

READER/CUSTOMER CARE SURVEY

We care about your opinions. Please take a moment to fill out this Reader Survey card and mail it back to us. As a special **"thank you"** we'll send you exciting news about interesting books and a valuable **Gift Certificate.**

Please PRINT using ALL CAPS

First Name _____ MI. ____ Last Name _____

Address _____

ST _____ Zip _____ City _____

Phone # (___) _____ Email: _____ Fax # (___) _____ Comments:

(1) Gender:
_____ Female _____ Male

(2) Age:
_____ 12 or under _____ 40-59
_____ 13-19 _____ 60+
_____ 20-39

(3) What attracts you most to a book?
(Please rank 1-4 in order of preference.)

	1	2	3	4
3) Title	○	○	○	○
4) Cover Design	○	○	○	○
5) Author	○	○	○	○
6) Content	○	○	○	○

(7) Where do you usually buy books?
Please fill in your top TWO choices.

1) _____ Bookstore
2) _____ Religious Bookstore
3) _____ Online
4) _____ Book Club/Mail Order
5) _____ Price Club (Costco, Sam's Club, etc.)
6) _____ Retail Store (Target, Wal-Mart, etc.)

SB1

NO POSTAGE
NECESSARY
IF MAILED
IN THE
UNITED STATES

BUSINESS REPLY MAIL
FIRST-CLASS MAIL   PERMIT NO 45   DEERFIELD BEACH, FL

POSTAGE WILL BE PAID BY ADDRESSEE

SIMCHA PRESS
3201 SW 15TH STREET
DEERFIELD BEACH FL 33442-9875

I..Ial..Il..I.I..IIIl.Ial..I.al..I.I.I.I

Just a Roll of the Eyes

A neighbor of mine shared the following story:

I have been working very hard at not speaking badly about people and not listening to gossip and negative talk, but I really blew it the other day. Someone asked me what I thought of the party that we had both attended the night before, and I told him I couldn't say. He laughed and said he agreed it was a lousy party. I hadn't said that at all! But he wasn't stupid—it was what I said, because it implied what I didn't say. He got it all right, and I got the lesson loud and clear.

You can even transgress the laws of speech without a sound coming out of your mouth! It's not hard to imagine. Picture two cool teenage girls standing together in the school hall. Suddenly another girl, dressed very unfashionably, walks by. One cool girl turns to the other and rolls her eyes. The other nods in agreement. Look out!

Body language, a roll of the eyes, a wince, a scowl, a smirk—they can all be destructive when done at the expense of another.

The Power of the Written Word

An entire industry exists based on evil speech that is not spoken—it is written. The most popular publications in the world (they are found, among other places, at your grocery store checkout line) are based on gossip and slander. But don't blame them. They only exist because we buy them.

One of the people in this world who Bob had long and greatly admired (whose name will remain nameless for reasons you will soon discover) passed away. Much had been written regarding this righteous person and the great works he had accomplished in his long and illustrious life.

Bob was happily doing some research on this person via the Internet when he came across a rather odd Web site that appeared to be "dedicated" to revealing the actual "truth" about this person, which was far different from the public's general perception. These revelations, from a person with presumably firsthand knowledge of the situation, included allegations that painted a picture of a cold, unkind, uncaring, bureaucratic despot who was not anything close to his public persona.

Did Bob believe it? Absolutely not! But he couldn't help thinking "What if it's true? At least some of it. After all, who really knows, and why would that person write it if not true? After all, what benefit would people have in making a claim that would result in hatred toward him by many?"

Does Bob believe it today? No. It can't be true. No way! But, what if—? And now, thanks to the gossip written and posted on the Internet about this saintly person, Bob can't help but have some creeping doubts despite the fact that he truly does not want to. His memory of this amazing person is forever clouded with doubt. He continues to do his best not to believe a single word of the totally unproven allegations. But that's difficult.

Remember: Evil speech can continue to kill a reputation long after a truly great person has died.

How Good Words Can Cause Destruction

So you think that avoiding negative talk can absolve you of breaking these laws, but even speaking positively about someone could be the beginning of a transgression. Consider the following shared with me by a friend:

Someone in my immediate family hates someone in my extended family—it's been going on for decades.

Try as I might, I can't seem to bring about peace between these people. After having a baby, the person in my extended family came to visit and brought a baby gift. We had a lovely time. I so appreciated her taking the time to visit and the generosity of her present.

The next time I saw the person in my immediate family, I took the opportunity to tell about the visit and present, hoping that it would somehow bring positive feelings and be a step toward peace.

As soon as I brought up my visitor's name, I could see the smoke coming out of the other person's ears. I responded by showing the lovely gift and praising how she had gone out of her way to visit. This was a big mistake. It was taking the plug out of a dam, and the flood of evil words came bursting forth.

I learned a powerful lesson—even positive speech can backfire into destructive speech.

This idea that you have to be careful even about saying something positive applies to many situations.

Think Before You Speak

What's wrong with telling your stepsister that your mom visited? Perhaps your mother rarely visits her, and the truth may be hurtful. Be sensitive. Perhaps she feels left out. Jewish tradition recognizes that one should be very careful with all associations, but especially potentially volatile family ties, such as everyone with "in-law" or "step" in their names.

Stop. Think. Look both ways before you speak.

> *Speak clearly, if you speak at all;*
> *carve every word before you let it fall.*
>
> Oliver Wendell Holmes

11

The Sixth Pathway: Modesty Is the Best Policy—Avoid Envy and Arrogance

Modesty is the conscience of the body.

Honoré de Balzac

To the Source

In the Book of Numbers in the Bible, we have a perplexing event referred to as Korach's rebellion. Moses had led the Jewish people out of Egypt and through the Sea of Reeds (also referred to as the Red Sea) to national revelation at Mount Sinai. He also had led them in victory against warring enemies in the desert, yet some of the men, led then by Korach, wanted to take over the leadership from Moses and his brother, Aaron.

> *They gathered together against Moses and against Aaron and said to them, "It is too much for you! For the entire assembly—all of them—are holy and God is among them; why do you exalt yourselves over the congregation of God?"* [38]

Who was Korach, and what could possibly motivate him to do such a deed? The Bible describes him as someone very rich and prestigious. He seems to have it all. And he was correct: Everyone, made in the image of God, is holy. But there was a flaw in Korach's argument, and you can see that in Moses' response:

> *"In the morning God will make known the one who is His own and the holy one, and He will draw him close to Himself, and whomever He will choose, He will draw close to Himself. ...Then the man whom God will choose—he is the holy one."* [39]

Korach omitted an essential factor in Israel's holiness. It is true that everyone is innately holy, but there is another aspect of holiness that depends on a person's merit. The greater a person works on self-improvement and actualizes his or her true potential, the greater the degree of holiness. In all his speeches in the Book of Numbers, Korach refers only to the communal, common holiness. Moses speaks of the individual God chooses. True leadership depends on merit, something Moses and Aaron possessed and Korach and his followers did not.

Korach and his followers had wealth, and they had prestige, but their downfall was their envy of Moses and Aaron. This blinded them—as envy does—to knowing what God really wants: what God wants, not what people want because someone else has it.

In the end the earth opens up and swallows alive Korach and his partisans, their wealth and their families.

Envy is destructive. Its root is arrogance, its symptom evil speech.

Avoid Envy

When you speak about your possessions or the possessions of others, or anyone's accomplishments, be careful that you do not do so in a way that would cause someone to become envious. "Oh, did you see the new home they bought?" "My spouse just got a big promotion!" Perhaps the person you are speaking to still lives in a modest apartment and their spouse has just been laid off.

It is considered praiseworthy to be very modest and low-key about your accomplishments, your possessions, your blessings and so on. These are all gifts from God, and they are to be used only for good. So use them—don't abuse them.

Imagine you gave your kid a brand-new red sports car for her sixteenth birthday. What if she was thrilled, took the keys, and spent the next few weeks driving around the neighborhood, showing off, and cutting classes? If you could, what would you do? You would take away the car!

God gives us so much: every dollar, every morsel of food, our looks, our health, our possessions and more. If we abuse these gifts and the result brings envy into the world, you never know, He might just take them away.

So when something beautiful happens or a blessing appears, if we find ourselves talking about it, we must speak in a manner to remind ourselves, and remind the person we are talking to, that this should only be used for good and should never cause envy in the world.

According to Jewish tradition, people would say something positive about someone, their looks, their achievements, and so on, and end with the phrase "without an evil eye" *(kanayna hora),* which means "without envy." People were careful to remind themselves and the listener that a good thing should never cause envy. Where there is envy, there is sure to be evil speech.

Many years ago when Bob was living in the Midwest, a young man came to town and made a fortune in oil. His was the classic "rags-to-riches" story, in which the man arrived with nothing and amassed great wealth through diligence and hard work. Bob was speaking with some people known to be friends of this person, and he asked them to tell the man's story. Bob, who was always fascinated by what he considered to be all-American-type success stories, had no idea that what he was really asking was for these people to speak evil at the man's expense.

Bob was told that although the man had come into town without money of his own, he had a wealthy uncle. The uncle, according to these "friends," introduced him to his buddy, who owned an oil company. The oil baron took on the penniless nephew as his personal protégé and helped the young man build a fortune of his own. "This young man," concluded the friends, was not necessarily a good businessman but, instead, simply "very, very lucky."

These quasi-friends themselves were not financially successful and obviously harbored within themselves a lot of envy. After all, why else would they share that view of their friend (even if factual) with Bob? (Remember, too, that whether or not what they said is true, speaking it is still destructive and wrong.)

The envious man thinks that if his neighbor breaks a leg, he will be able to walk better himself.

Helmut Schoeck

Avoid Arrogance

It is easier to put an ox into an eggcup than for a man full of conceit to receive wisdom.

Ernest Bramah (Smith)

The root of a lot of destructive speech can also be found within arrogance. Maimonides said that arrogance is the absolutely worst character trait to possess. Jewish mysticism, known as Kabbalah, states that an arrogant person has no share in the world to come, no place in heaven or eternity. Arrogant people are so full of themselves that there's no room for others, and certainly no room for God. An arrogant person thinks he or she *is* God.

The best character trait to possess is the opposite of arrogance: humility. However, in modern Western thought, humility is not something people seem to strive for or admire.

Imagine you are in my home, and I tell you that the humblest man who ever lived is coming to meet you. How would such a man knock on the door? Would he knock softly and quietly? How would he enter? Would he be bent over, looking meek and shuffling in unobtrusively to find a chair in the corner and sit as still as a mouse? If he spoke, would it be barely a whisper, making no eye contact whatsoever?

Well, erase all that from your mind, because according to Biblical tradition, Moses was the humblest man who ever lived. Moses!? Why he was the one who stood up to Pharaoh! Do you think he whispered, "Uhm, if it isn't too much trouble, could you possibly let God's people go?"

No! He stood strong and spoke firmly with confidence, "Let God's people go!!" And then throughout the forty years in the desert, he led the Jewish people to be victorious in war. This was no meek and mild man.

Then why does the Torah refer to him as the epitome of humility?

Because humility does not derive from thinking "I'm nothing." Rather, real humility stems from thinking "I'm something—but I know where it is all from—I know the source of all my talents, skills and success. In the end, it's all from God."

But this creates confusion within us. How can everything be from God? Didn't I earn my degree with my own hard work? Don't I have a right to be proud of that accomplishment? Yes, but don't take pride, take pleasure—because where pride lives, arrogance lurks.

You got your degree? Congratulations! What are you so proud of: That you were born into a time of world history when people like yourself are allowed to seek higher education? That you were born into a country that has such opportunity? That you are from the small percentage of families for whom the means and opportunity to go to college or university are available?

Yes, you worked hard. Take pleasure in that. But don't be proud of the fact that God gave you an opportunity and you took it. You would have been remiss not to!

Let me give you another example. I was working with a young boy a while back and trying to get this very point across to him. I asked him what he is good at that he is proud of. He told me he's a really good hockey player.

Then I said, "Imagine that you received a birthday check in the mail from your great aunt. And the next day you told me the following: 'Guess what? You won't believe this! Yesterday I got a check in the mail. I had to read the envelope, recognize that it was for me and carefully open up the envelope. I had to take out the contents, see it was a check and put it into my wallet. I had to open the door, walk out of my house and walk to the corner bank. I had to open up the bank door, walk inside, stand in line, wait my turn and go up to the teller. I had to lift a pen, sign my name on the back of the check, slide it over to the teller and wait while she processed the check. Then I had to open my hand, take the money, put it into my wallet, turn and walk out the door. *I am so proud of myself! Look what I did!'* And of course, I am thinking, 'Brother, you'd be crazy not to cash the check! What are you so proud of?'"

When we use our minds, bodies, talents and skills properly, we are just cashing the check that God wrote to us. Our achievements are garnered with hard work, not with simplistic stories about going to the bank. I explained to the bar mitzvah boy that when he is playing hockey really well, he is exerting tremendous effort, but in the end he is cashing the check. God gave him a healthy body, he was born into a family that has the means to allow him to join hockey leagues, he was born into a country where hockey is played and encouraged, he was born into a time of the world when thirteen-year-old boys don't have to work in the fields to support their families and instead can freely play sports after school.

He got it. Now when he plays, he doesn't take pride, he takes pleasure. He knows he is a good player, but he now also realizes the Source of it all. Yes, he chose to use his gifts properly—that's the pleasure. He could have chosen to use his physical prowess to be a bully in the school yard. Instead he is channeling it into healthy sportsmanship. Pleasure, not pride.

When you are thankful for what you have, you are unlikely to ever open the doors to envy. Tapping into humility will open the door to a life of positive energy and surely positive speech. You will never begrudge anyone anything. It will be a life without envy, a life of pure pleasure.

Without humility there can be no humanity.

John Buchan

12

The Seventh Pathway: Beware of Repeating Information—Or, Loose Lips Sink Ships

*None are so fond of secrets as those
who do not mean to keep them.*

Charles Caleb Cotton

To the Source

The laws of speech also address when it is proper and when it is improper to repeat information.

The Bible says, "And God spoke to Moses, telling him to say to the Jewish people. . . ."[40] God is giving Moses permission to repeat the information He speaks. From this we learn that unless someone gives you specific permission to repeat something, you are not allowed to repeat it.

Even if the person didn't preface the information with the disclaimer "Don't repeat this," you must assume you are not allowed to say it. Only when you have explicit permission can you share with others what you have been told.

In the Garden of Eden, the downfall of Adam and Eve occurred over this exact issue. God said to them:

> *"Of every tree of the garden you may freely eat; but of the Tree of Knowledge of Good and Evil, you must not eat thereof; for on the day you eat of it, you shall surely die. . . ."*[41]
>
> *Now the serpent was cunning beyond any beast of the field that God had made. He said to Eve, "Did, perhaps, God say: 'You shall not eat of any tree of the garden?'"*

> *Eve said to the serpent, "Of the fruit of any tree of the gar-*
> *den we may eat. Of the fruit of the tree which is in the center*
> *of the garden God has said: 'You shall neither eat it nor touch*
> *it, lest you die.'"*
>
> *The serpent said to the woman, "You will surely not die; for*
> *God knows that on the day you eat of it your eyes will be*
> *opened and you will be like God, knowing good and bad."*
>
> *And the woman perceived that the tree was good for eat-*
> *ing and that it was a delight to the eyes ... and she took of its*
> *fruit and ate; and she gave also to her husband with her and*
> *he ate.*[42]

We know how the story turns out. Adam and Eve are caught and punished, and we have been paying for it ever since. Man now has to work for a living, and woman will have pain in having children, and so on.

It all began because Eve repeated information God had told her, *without His permission.* Not only did she repeat it, but she repeated it to the wrong creation, to the serpent. Not only did she repeat it to the serpent, but she embellished it. She added to what God had originally said. He had told them not to eat from the tree, but when she repeated it, she said that God had said not to eat it or *touch* it.

This is what can happen when we break the confidentiality clause. This is not just a clause for clergy, physicians and lawyers. It is a clause that applies to all of humanity, forever binding.

> *A dear friend of Bob (we'll call him Tom) falls under the cate-*
> *gory of one who tends to repeat practically everything he hears,*
> *and generally seems to do so to the wrong person at the wrong*

time. Eventually, Bob had to choose his words to the point of discomfort and stop saying anything to or around his friend that could ever possibly hurt another's feelings if taken out of context.

This had nothing to do with Bob speaking badly about others, but was simply a matter of conveying information that needed to be stated to Tom (or something that Tom might hear from someone else).

For example, Bob stopped doing business with a business owner who was a friend of a friend because his product wasn't up to par. When Bob and Tom stopped in at a competitor's store to buy that product, Tom asked Bob why he no longer patronized the previous business owner, the friend of a friend. In order not to speak badly, Bob simply said that he hadn't done business with him for a while but that, because of the infrequency of his purchases of that particular product, it didn't really matter.

Well, you can guess that Tom somehow managed to mention all of this to the friend of the business owner. When Bob was asked by this person why he stopped patronizing his friend, Bob was put into the position of having to defend himself by explaining the deficiency of the product.

Bob was angry again at Tom for saying what simply never needed to be said. Tom could not understand what the problem was, and still doesn't to this day.

Perhaps Tom would be best served by learning a saying from the Talmudic sages: "What is man's greatest art in this world? To act as if he is mute."[43]

Even if something seems innocent and innocuous, you cannot repeat it. For example, what's wrong with telling your cousin that your neighbor is thinking of putting his house up for sale and moving to another state? Perhaps that neighbor works in the same firm as the cousin, and the boss does not know this person is leaving town. Imagine the trouble that could happen if this simple fact suddenly got out. Instead of leaving on good terms, the neighbor could be fired, all because you repeated a simple fact! What seems like nothing to you could mean everything to another. Think before you speak.

However, in some situations it is reasonable to repeat information. If you are privy to something that was said to a group of three or more people in a very public way, and no disclaimer was made, you can assume it is in the public realm and you could theoretically repeat it.

But be careful out there. And please, be sensitive to other people. You were told that so-and-so is pregnant, and that information was told to a group of people in a very public way—so what's wrong with telling others? Perhaps the person you are running to tell is struggling with infertility. Announcing with glee another person's pregnancy could be very hurtful. I have a friend who suffered for years because of infertility, and she told me that every time someone announced to her that someone else was pregnant, she pretended to be happy, but it was really another knife in her heart.

Be sensitive—you never know what is going on in another person's life. As the saying goes, it's better to be safe than sorry. Stop and think before you speak. If you are not sure if you have permission to repeat something, assume you don't. You can always check and say it later.

Your personal "default setting" is confidentiality.

Rabbi Yaakov Meyer of Denver, Colorado

The Danger of Elevator Talk

I f you live in a city where people still greet one another in the elevator and exchange pleasantries about the weather, you know what "elevator talk" is—nothing deep or complex, just chat that fills the empty space.

Be careful of this in, and outside, the elevator. Sometimes we say things just to fill the pregnant pauses in conversation, and we say things we really shouldn't. Idle chatter about nothing can lead to something.

Remember the adage "Loose lips sink ships"? You do not want people speaking about you and your business, so do others a favor and don't speak about them. You never know what kind of damage can result.

Of every ten persons who talk about you,
nine will say something bad, and the tenth
will say something good in a bad way.

Antoine Rivarol

13

The Eighth Pathway: Honesty Really Is the Best Policy— Most of the Time

*True speech is established forever,
but a false tongue is only for a moment.*

Proverbs 12:19

*I don't give them hell. I just tell the truth
and they think it is hell.*

Harry Truman

J ewish tradition teaches that when God signs His name, He signs it "Truth."[44] Of course, God doesn't really sign His name, but the message is clear—to the Almighty, truth is everything. We, created in the image of God, must be very careful to always speak the truth. However, speaking the "plain" truth can be damaging at times. It might generate the grave cost of hurting someone's feelings or violating his or her dignity. We have to balance that against the obligation to speak the truth.

Following are some important guidelines when weighing these "white lies." Sometimes truth can cause more damage than truth is worth. Let's examine some of these areas where "nothing but the whole truth" should not apply.

1. For peace

*People who are brutally honest get more
satisfaction out of the brutality than the honesty.*

Richard J. Needham

To the Source

In the Book of Genesis, God reveals himself to Sarah and tells her that she will have a child. She laughs and adds incredulously, "After I have withered, shall I again have delicate skin? [In other words, 'I'm too old!'] And my husband is old!" Then God appears before Abraham, and Abraham asks Him why Sarah is laughing. God tells Abraham, "She is laughing because I told her she would have a child and she said how can I have a child when I am so old?"[45]

In a sense, God actually lied to Abraham. He left out the fact that Sarah also said that Abraham is too old. He did so for peace in the home, peace between a husband and a wife.

Sometimes for the sake of peace, harmony and a good marriage, one is allowed to "change your words."[46]

Another story tells of a man who goes to the wedding of a friend. His friend, the groom, runs up to him before the ceremony and points out his bride. "Isn't she beautiful?" he asks. In the physical sense of the word, by almost anyone's opinion, she is not.

The question is, what should the man answer?

There are two main schools of thought, according to the Talmud. One is the outlook that one should praise other aspects of the bride. "Wow, she looks, really, uh, strong. You won't have any trouble at harvest time, you lucky guy."

The other school of thought says to lie. Tell him she is beautiful—praise every feature. (Besides, by saying she is beautiful you are not—technically—lying. After all, to the groom, she *is* beautiful!)

We would do well to follow the latter school of thought on this matter.[47] Jewish law states that you don't even have to search for double entendres so that what you say is technically true. Why? If your friend really cared what you thought about his bride, when would he have asked you? *Before* he asked her to marry him. Now that it is a done deal (or minutes away from one) is not the time for honesty; this is the time to be kind. Your friend does not want your opinion, he wants your *confirmation.* Do not hurt his feelings. Give him what he wants.

If your friend comes to you from the hairdresser and asks how you like her new haircut, and it looks like it's been hacked off, this is also a time to be kind. Tell her you love it. After all, what is she going to do, glue her hair back on? Next time she is looking like she needs a new cut, though, suggest your stylist or point out a flattering style in a magazine.

If your friends invite you over to see their newly decorated home and it's orange and purple from top to bottom, there is no benefit in telling them that it makes you nauseous. If they really wanted your opinion, they would have consulted you before they chose the décor. Your goal now is to spare their feelings. Tell them you love it. Tell them it's tasteful and beautiful. Tell them that and more, because their feelings are more important than anything, even truth.

If you have two friends who are not speaking, you can go to one and say the other one wants to patch things up, even though they don't. Then you can go to the other one and do the same. Ideally they will now meet and make peace. You bent the truth in order to make it happen. That's okay. The Almighty wants peace.

Remember, though, to think through your game plan. While your intentions to create peace may be indisputably honorable, they can backfire if not handled correctly. For instance, if you tell each friend that the other wants to patch things up, and then one says to the other, "I'm glad you told Bob you wanted to patch things up," the other might become angry. He could say, "It was you who knew you were wrong," and then the bad feelings begin anew. This will, of course, have the opposite effect of what you intended.

Is It Okay to Lie Instead of Hurting Someone's Feelings? Yes!

One of Bob's favorite episodes of the famous *I Love Lucy* show involved a wager between Lucy and her best friend, Ethel. Apparently, Lucy had gotten into the habit of lying and Ethel wanted to help break her of the habit. Ethel bet that Lucy couldn't keep from telling a lie for a certain period of time (as Bob recalls, it was for one week).

The next scene had the two friends attending a party, and then their friend walked into the room. Safely out of earshot, Lucy and Ethel confided in each other that the woman's hat was quite unattractive. In fact, Lucy defined it as something one might see as part of a "nightmare." (Lucy's use of destructive speech will trap her!)

As the woman approached Lucy and Ethel, she almost immediately asked them what they thought of her new hat. Ethel simply lied (she wasn't chained by the terms of the bet) and commented on how delightful it was.

Sensing her opportunity to win the bet, Ethel asked Lucy what *she* thought of the hat.

After stammering a bit in order to find some words that wouldn't hurt the woman's feelings while still not lying, Lucy finally said, "I told Ethel it was something you'd see in a 'dream.'" (Ahh, she didn't lie. A nightmare *is* a type of dream.) Ethel had Lucy trapped, though, and asked her to state the exact words she had used, which Lucy then admitted. Lucy and Ethel's friend was, of course, hurt, after which Ethel explained the situation.

We learn two lessons here. The first is that if you don't speak badly about others in the first place, there's a good chance you'll never be caught in a situation where something you say will unnecessarily hurt someone's feelings. Had Lucy not said what she did about the hat, Ethel could not have used that as a weapon. Sure, it is just a sitcom, but you can probably think of similar situations that have come back to haunt you.

Of course there are times when we must lovingly point out to someone that their actions or behavior need correction. But if you have to do it, do it with tact and diplomacy.

Consider this example: Emily has been trying to lose a lot of weight. Thus far she has lost five pounds, but that hasn't yet made a significant difference in the way she looks. In conversation she asks, "So, do I look any thinner yet?" What do you say? If you tell her the complete truth, she might become discouraged enough to stop trying and to grab a piece of chocolate cake to make herself feel better. Instead, you might say, "You know, there's some progress." (Actually, that's not even a fib—

there *is* progress; you just can't see it yet!) This gives her the strength to continue her quest to lose weight, look better and become healthier. Would it have helped her for you to have told her the truth, the whole truth and nothing but the truth? Doubtful. Of course, again, it's important to take into consideration the situation and the individual.

> *The pure and simple truth*
> *is rarely pure and never simple.*

Oscar Wilde

We can also learn from this story about a man I'll call Steven. Lately, he has been snapping impatiently at his friends. When one of his friends, Annie, mentions this to him, he denies it, obviously not even aware of this new, unwelcome trait. Terry, another of his friends, would like to help him lose this behavior before it becomes a habit and other people choose to stop hanging around with him. But he also knows that Steven is not always receptive to criticism. Telling him right out that he's been insulting and snappy will most likely not persuade Steven to change. Instead, Terry decides to take another road. He'll praise Steven for his patience and kindness, the very qualities he wants his friend to regain.

When Steven reacts negatively to someone, Terry says, "Steven, that's not like you. You're one of the most patient people I know." Or, during a moment when Steven is not acting negatively, Terry might comment, "Steven, one thing I really admire about you is your kindness and patience with people." If this is what it takes to reach someone like Steven, it is the correct manner of doing so. Again, judge the situation according to the individual, and define the best way to help him or her.

Keep in mind that you must have no manipulative interest in doing this. This is not empty flattery; this is trying to help another person to change for the good.

2. For privacy and personal dignity

Truth itself hath not the privilege to be employed at all times and in every kind: Be her use never so noble, it hath its circumscriptions and limits.

Michel Eyquem de Montaigne

The Bible respects a person's right to privacy and personal dignity. If you are asked a question and the truthful answer would violate your privacy, you may "change the truth" to protect yourself. This applies only in a case where the inquirer has no right to ask the question. If someone from the bank where you're applying for a loan asks you about your income, he or she has a right to a truthful answer, whereas a curious friend does not.

If someone asks you something that is private and you'd like it to remain that way, simply respond in a tactful and kind way that is also noncommittal. For example, Dave asks if you're going to go in on that new hot deal that John's been talking up. Just say something along the lines of, "John's a great guy; I just make it a personal policy not to discuss my investments, either way. But thanks for asking." Here you've provided absolutely no clue as to your decision, while not hurting Dave's feelings. The bonus is that you've also taught Dave that it isn't polite to ask these kinds of questions in the first place. Whether Dave "gets it" or not is another story, but at least you've done your part when it comes to positive speech.

On the other hand, answering in an impolite and purposely hurtful way, such as, "It's none of your business!" will probably do more in tipping your hand and helping Dave to deduce the answer more than anything else you could say.

So, like always, being kind is not only the right way to be, but is also the best way to accomplish your goal; in this case, keeping your personal business . . . personal.

3. To minimize your accomplishments

It is better to deserve honors and not have them,
than to have them and not deserve them.

Mark Twain

A friend says, "I heard you ran that fund-raiser all by yourself!" In fact, you did run that fund-raiser all by yourself. You are allowed to say, "Actually, it was a group effort." You can give credit to your colleagues. You know what you did. God knows what you did. You are allowed to play down the facts.

You want honor? The sages ask, "Who is honored?" The answer? "The one who flees from honor."[48]

A man once told a rabbi, "I don't understand. I am always running from honor, and yet I am never honored."

"My son," answered the rabbi, "it's because when you are running, you are always looking over your shoulder."

14

The Ninth Pathway: Learn to Say "I'm Sorry"—Or, "Okay, So I Blew It. Now What?"

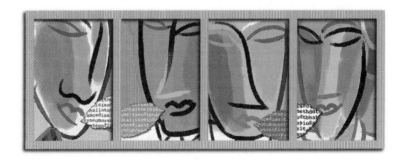

Most people repent their sins by thanking
God they ain't so wicked as their neighbors.

Josh Billings

To the Source

The famous story in Genesis about the two sons of Adam and Eve—Cain and Abel—teaches us an eternal lesson about mistakes and our reaction to them.

Abel became a shepherd, and Cain became a tiller of the land.

After a period of time, Cain brought an offering to God of the fruit of the ground, and as for Abel, he also brought of the firstlings of his flock and from their choicest. God turned to Abel and to his offering, but to Cain and to his offering He did not turn. This annoyed Cain exceedingly, and his countenance fell.

And God said to Cain, "Why are you annoyed, and why has your countenance fallen? Surely if you improve yourself, you will be forgiven. But if you do not improve yourself, sin rests at the door. Its desire is toward you, yet you can conquer it."[49]

Let's examine this more closely. Clearly Cain has fallen out of favor in God's eyes. He made an offering to Him, but it wasn't on the higher level that his brother Abel had made. Cain offered some simple produce, while Abel took the first and best of his flock for God. God does not need produce or livestock, for He has no needs. He's got it all. The offerings are not for Him, but for us. It was the way we would express our love and gratitude to God. Without it, we would miss out on the deep pleasure of appreciating that everything is from the Almighty.

Clearly Cain's feelings of appreciation were not on the same level as Abel's, and God's reaction illustrated that.

Cain had made a mistake, and he reacted by getting angry and depressed. God told him that this was not the appropriate reaction to a mistake. Instead, he should learn from mistakes and become a better person—in this case, a person who feels more appreciation and gratitude for all their blessings and abundance.

Does Cain listen? No, and this is what happens next:

> Cain spoke with his brother, Abel, and it happened when they were in the field, that Cain rose up against his brother Abel and killed him.
>
> God said to Cain, "Where is Abel your brother?" (as if God doesn't know)
>
> And he said, "I don't know. Am I my brother's keeper?"[50]

When you make a mistake, you can learn a lot by admitting it, saying you are sorry and taking the appropriate punishment. God was giving Cain a second opportunity to own up to his mistakes and to change. But Cain just didn't get it. His lack of remorse regarding the first mistake, and his lack of desire to change, resulted in even greater sin. God gave him the opportunity to admit his mistake and change. And Cain not only refused to do it, but he threw it all back on God. *"Am I my brother's keeper?"* He might as well have been saying, "Hey, God, don't blame me, you're supposed to be taking care of everyone!"

A friend of mine shared the following:

I have four kids, and the two middle ones fight like cats and dogs. This is how the scenario often goes: I hear commotion in the den, shouting and carrying on. Then I hear a cry that clearly indicates someone is hurt. I run into the den and find that it is my two middle ones at it again. They have argued over a toy, and one has hit the other. Of course I admonish the perpetrator and say, "Tell your brother you are sorry." He turns to his brother and says sarcastically, "Sorry." I tell him never to do that again, and I leave.

Needless to say, the depth of his remorse does not bring tears to my eyes, and I know it is just a matter of time before it will certainly happen again.

Let's apply our desire to speak positively of others to this example. Speaking evil is a terrible mistake, but let's approach these lapses in judgment in the right way. How should we feel when we make a mistake, and how can we make it right?

First of all, know that everyone makes mistakes, and when it comes to violating God's commandments, everyone trips on this one. It's hard to feel proud of the fact that you didn't murder anyone today or steal (hopefully). After all, these are choices that don't cross our paths too often (again, hopefully).

Yet because we speak every day, sometimes every minute, the chance of us slipping up and saying things we are not supposed to is pretty high. Even among people who are aware of these laws and strive not to break them, there are campaigns to stop evil speech. There are "Drive Away Gossip" bumper stickers; "Is this gossip?" stickers to put on your phones (let's face it—90 percent of gossip probably happens on the phone); and community campaigns to put this destructive habit to rest.

You get a good feeling when among people who are working on this. Here's another story from my own life:

I was working day and night on a major fund-raising campaign for a religious nonprofit organization. One of the temp staff worked very late hours with me. One night, after a very long and hard day, we were again up and working. At one point she started speaking badly about someone else who worked there but had gone home for the day. I didn't react and just kept working. She started up again, but I didn't grab the bait.

Finally I turned to her and said, "Jane, you're a temp worker, so you have been in many offices, right?"

"Right," she answered.

"Tell me, what's different about working here than any other place you have ever worked?"

She thought for a moment, and then said, "Here, people don't talk about one another. There's no office gossip."

My husband, a rabbi, was learning with someone who told him that he liked hanging out with us because, he said, "When I walk out of the room, I know you are not going to talk about me." In his social circles, that was unique.

So what do we do if we trip up and make a mistake? First of all, know that everyone makes mistakes. The Bible is filled with people, even some great people, who made mistakes.

Moses himself was not allowed to enter the Land of Israel because of a mistake. Miriam, his sister, spoke badly of Moses, which resulted in her being struck with "tzaras," a leprous-like affliction.

As you can see, people in the Bible were humans, made of flesh and blood. Though many achieved greatness, they also made mistakes.

> *For there is no man so wholly righteous on Earth*
> *that he (always) does good and never sins.*
>
> Ecclesiastes 7:20

Return

What does God want from us when we make mistakes? To do *teshuvah,* which means "return." But what are we returning to?

Let's say you need to make a quick trip to Chicago. So, you book your round-trip ticket from your local airport to Chicago and then back home again. When you come home, you "return," do you not? Returning means coming back to somewhere you've been, somewhere familiar. Return after making a moral mistake means returning to the good person we know we have been and can become again. We are remembering that we are not just bodies, but also souls.

We all know when we stray, rationalize, bend the truth, avoid the effort, and ignore what is really important and meaningful in our lives. Mistakes come in all shapes and sizes. Often we know at the time that we shouldn't be doing what we are doing, but we are caught up, distracted and convinced that somehow at the moment it is right.

God understands that, just as parents don't expect their kids to be perfect. You know as they grow they will make mistakes. Even when you tell them not to do something that will harm them, they do it anyway.

How do you want them to feel when they err? Weighed down by guilt for life? Terrible about themselves? Of course not. You want them to recognize that they have made a mistake, to stop making it, to make it good, to learn from it and to go on. This is not guilt; guilt is paralyzing and self-absorbing. The idea is to use mistakes to grow.

God is our Father in Heaven. He doesn't want us to be weighed down by negativity and self-loathing when we make mistakes. When we make the wrong choices in life, they should be seen as opportunities for growth, not as chains and shackles to restrain us forever.

Following are the steps for return set out by Maimonides.[51] When we make a mistake, we are to go through the process step-by-step. The result is forgiveness and growth.

Since we are dealing with evil speech, let's use it as an example. (You can always remember these four steps by starting with the acronym RSVP; just flip the first two letters so the acronym becomes SRVP).

Step 1: *Stop.* Stop making the mistake. If you are gossiping, make the decision to stop.

Step 2: *Regret.* You should indeed feel regret for your error. It's indisputably wrong to gossip. You are hurting so many people by doing it, including yourself.

Step 3: *Verbalize*. Say you are sorry, out loud, to God. This doesn't have to be done at a house of worship, it doesn't have to be on an especially holy day and it doesn't have to happen in any particular language. Talk to God. Speak aloud, at least in an audible whisper (not silently). Tell Him you are sorry, that He gave you the gift of speech and you used it in a terrible way.

If the mistake harmed other people (as opposed to being a mistake between you and God, like using His name in vain), you have to make amends with that other person.

In the case of destructive speech, chances are you hurt plenty of people. Think back to previous chapters in which we discussed the people being harmed—you, the person you are speaking about and, most of all, the listener. In order to complete the return, you have to go to the people you wronged *before* you go to God. God does not forgive us until we have cleared it up with people first.

Imagine you spoke badly about George to Mary. First you have to go to Mary and tell her you were gossiping to her, tell her it was wrong to do so and ask her please not to believe what you said. Ask her to forgive you for putting her into such a position.

Here comes the really hard part: Now you have to go to George—who may never have heard that you spoke about him—and ask his forgiveness.

Can you imagine how difficult that would be? How ashamed would you feel, having to apologize to someone for speaking badly about them? If we only lived with this understanding about the way to clear up the mistake of speaking badly of another, how much more careful we would be before opening our mouths.

However, do not go to George and tell him you spoke badly about him if it would hurt him too badly or even enrage him. If he would demand to know to whom you spoke, and you told him you spoke to Mary, and the result would be that now he would not talk to you *or* Mary—well, that is not what God wants.

If you absolutely know that coming clean and telling George would result in more strife, either for him or others, then you are allowed to clear it up in the way described in the next paragraph. Remember, though, that this is not the optimum way of doing it, and when you use this alternative, you must know in your heart that you are taking the easy way out.

Here's how it works: Go through the first steps of return (SRV). When you get to step 3 (verbalize), go to Mary and apologize, and then go to George and say the following: "You know, George, I've been thinking about how important your friendship is to me, and I just want to say that if there has ever been anything that I have ever said or done to offend you, please forgive me." Hopefully, George will answer, "Hey, no sweat, there's nothing. And if I have ever said or done anything to hurt you, forgive me, okay?"

Done. Yes, you took the easy way out, but you're done. The ideal is to be open and tell it straight, but if your goal is peace, do whatever it takes to achieve it.

Step 4: *Plan.* How can you be sure that the mistake won't happen again? Make a practical plan of action. If you know that speaking to a friend about certain subjects or people will definitely lead to evil speech, you could make a pact to avoid these subjects. A good plan to circumvent such a situation is to learn about the laws. At the end of this book, you will find an appendix reviewing these rules, as well as recommendations for further reading on this subject. Five minutes a day spent learning the laws of speech can make a dramatic difference in reducing the amount of gossip spoken.

Once you have completed these steps, God accepts your return, but it's still on the books, so to speak. Yes, it is noted that it was taken care of, but it's still there.

How do you completely edit it out? By going to the next step, called *teshuvah gamurah,* or "complete return" (another term provided us by Maimonides). This occurs after you have gone through the steps, time has passed, and God, sometimes with a very good sense of humor, puts you in the same position as when you originally made the mistake, and you do not repeat the mistake. When this occurs, not only are you forgiven, but it's as if you never made the original mistake. It is edited out of the story of your life, as if it had never happened.

Let's return to our example of speaking badly about George to Mary. Now you have done your return, gone through the four steps, and all is forgiven. Now it is six months later. You and Mary are at a cocktail party, and someone asks you about the latest escapades of your friend George. It's a heavenly setup (literally)! Did you learn your lesson the first time? You don't take the bait, and you shrug your shoulders and change the subject. All eyes and ears are on you, and you pass!

Complete return! It's as if you have never spoken about George in your life. You did it. You got it. You have truly returned to the good person you know you are. You have reconnected with the fact that you are a soul, and that every word counts; every word can either bring you closer to your Creator, or farther away.

Why do we not feel uplifted after spending an evening talking about others? It's because we chose to misuse our gift of speech. Each time we make that choice we are distancing ourselves, lowering ourselves, from the Ultimate.

If you ever feel far away from God, remember that He didn't move—you did. Your choice of words can provide that movement. Choose wisely.

God enters by a private door into every individual.

Ralph Waldo Emerson

God is in the details.

Albert Einstein

15

THE TENTH PATHWAY:
FORGIVE

The weak can never forgive.
Forgiveness is the attribute of the strong.

Mahatma Gandhi

An apology is the superglue of life.
It can repair just about anything.

Lynn Johnston

Sometimes it is harder to say "I forgive" than to say "I'm sorry."

People are limited, they are human and make mistakes, they had a whole life before encountering you, and they struggle with character flaws and challenges in their own lives (just like you). Awareness of this will help open you to forgiveness.

A lot of society's problems can be traced back to one cause: senseless hatred. Rabbi Noah Weinberg, dean of Aish HaTorah, defines senseless hatred as the following: when you hate someone because their mistakes are different from yours.

Sound familiar?

What is the antidote to such a thing? Love—not senseless love, but love with a purpose. Loving someone is a choice. How do people know that they will love their kids even before they are born? Perhaps they will turn out like the sniveling brats next door! They know because they made a choice to love. That choice involves seeing the virtues in a person, focusing on their virtues, identifying them with those virtues. The more you do this, the more you will feel love. Love isn't blind. You can love your kids and still see their mistakes. You choose to focus on their goodness.

When you are in this frame of mind, it's a lot easier to forgive. If a person has the virtues that you have been continually making the effort to see, when they err or disappoint you, it will be a lot easier to take—and ultimately to forgive.

What if you're the one asking for forgiveness? You hope the other person will forgive, but what if they don't? Your obligation is to try—to make three sincere attempts at apologizing. This means three *major* efforts. First try a personal apology. If the offended person rejects you, try writing a letter (that way you can articulate your apology just right and provide the opportunity for the other person to read and re-read and consider your request). If that doesn't work, employ the help of a third party, someone the other person respects, and see if he or she can broker a peaceful resolution.

People really do want to forgive, but factors like ego, past hurts, emotion, social pressure and insecurities often block the way. Yet anger and hatred eat up a person and hinder self-development and day-to-day happiness. It's like a black cloud hanging over one's head every moment of the day.

We can take a cue from former president Abraham Lincoln. During his presidency, our sixteenth chief executive was frustrated and angered by many, including those in his own cabinet, who didn't like him, and his generals, who were not following his orders. Lincoln often wrote scathing letters heaped with every vicious, cutting insult he could devise. But before he sent a letter—even after he'd seal it sometimes—he'd tear it up into tiny pieces and throw it in the trash. That's how he got all his negative feelings off his chest. Forgiveness means letting go.

To the Source

If you were Joseph and your brothers tried to kill you and then sold you away forever as a slave, how could you possibly forgive them? But Joseph does just that, as we see in the scene in the Book of Genesis where he reveals his true identity to his brothers.

> Then Joseph said to his brothers, "Come close to me, if you please," and they came close. And he said, "I am Joseph your brother—it is me who you sold into Egypt. And now, be not distressed, nor reproach yourselves for having sold me here, for it was to be a provider that God sent me ahead of you . . . to insure your survival in the land and to sustain you for a momentous deliverance. And now: It was not you who sent me here, but God."[52]

Joseph was so righteous, not only did he forgive his brothers for what they had done to him, but he reached the highest level of forgiveness, which is to realize that everything is a lesson and message from the Almighty, even the wrongs that people do to us. Joseph saw God's guiding hand in his life. If his brothers had not sold him as a slave, he would not have risen to such a position of power in Egypt, and then there would have been no way for his family to survive the famine.

> Hurry—go up to my father and say to him, "So said your son Joseph: 'God has made me master of all Egypt. Come down to me; do not delay. You will reside in the land of Goshen and you will be near to me—you, your sons, your grandchildren, your flock and your cattle, and all that is yours. And I will

provide for you there—for there will be five more years of famine—so you do not become destitute, you, your household, and all that is yours.'"[53]

I learned a lesson of forgiveness many years ago—certainly not on the level of Joseph, but still a big lesson:

When I was in my early twenties, single and living in Israel, I supported my studies by establishing a private aerobics business. At one point, one of my clients became very angry at me over something and for months we were not on speaking terms. Because I never talked to her about it, I really had no idea what it was all about. I also knew that this woman was under a lot of personal pressure. Yet it was a very uncomfortable situation, as you can imagine.

Time passed and it was now the day leading into Yom Kippur, the Day of Atonement. At sundown the holy day would begin. The heaviness of what was about to happen spiritually was in the air. This was the day during which one asked God for forgiveness, and the days leading up to it were called the Ten Days of Teshuvah, when forgiveness was in the air. Everyone would be examining their past deeds and relationships and making an effort to change for the good, for God does not forgive a person until they have first cleared up any conflicts with others.

The one matter hanging over my head was the conflict with this one woman. I had many errands that day and was on the run, yet I knew I couldn't enter into Yom Kippur with this unresolved. Even though I didn't think I had done anything wrong and that I was being treated unfairly by the woman, at a friend's house I picked up the phone and called and asked for forgiveness.

"Me, forgive you?" she said. "Why I've been trying to reach you all day! It's you who must forgive me. I am so sorry for how I treated you. I've just been under so many pressures. Thank you for calling. I don't know what I would have done if I hadn't reached you."

Sometimes people are desperate to forgive—but you have to be the one to exert the first effort and provide the opportunity.

It takes two to tango—two to create a conflict, and two to resolve it. Someone has to take the first step. It really can be you.

Where there is forgiveness, there is peace. Where there is no forgiveness, there is sure to be destructive speech.

> *I can forgive, but I cannot forget, is only another way of saying, I will not forgive.*
>
> Henry Ward Beecher

16

THE REVERSE
GOSSIP GAME

*You can tell more about a person
by what he says about others
than you can by what others say about him.*

Leo Aikman

The words "Seek peace and pursue it"[54] tell us not only to value peace, but to actually go out of our way to bring it about, both in our own relationships, and even in the relationships of other people. In other words, if there is a rift between two people, we should take it upon ourselves to do our best to heal it and bring about peace. Of course, only God can control whether or not this eventually happens, but we are obligated to make the effort.

With that in mind, I want to share one of the most effective ways to accomplish this. It's called The Reverse Gossip Game.

In this game, instead of telling people the gossip said about them or others, we repeat only the good that people say (even if we have to "suggest" that good), and we find reasons to judge others favorably in all other situations. Let's say, for instance, that John speaks negatively about Mary, for example:

John: Mary is really lazy.
You: I've never noticed that. She is talented, wouldn't you agree?
John (grudgingly): Yes, I guess so.

Later you see Mary at the coffee machine and the conversation goes as follows:

You: I was talking with John earlier. He was saying you are very talented (after all, he did agree to that, didn't he?).

Mary: Wow! I didn't know he thought that of me. I've always felt he was very judgmental and snobby.

You: Hmm, never picked up on that. Really hard worker, isn't he?

Mary: Well, I guess you have to give him credit for that.

The next day you and John are talking and you happen to mention your conversation with Mary:

You: Mary was talking about how hard a worker you are.

John: Really? Didn't think she liked me, but maybe she's not so bad after all.

The next time John and Mary cross paths they see each other in an entirely different light, with a completely different attitude and set of expectations—one of peace, enjoyment and kindness. And it all happened because of you.

You don't feel as though you've manipulated them, do you? There are people who might feel that way. Interesting, isn't it? It's perfectly acceptable to repeat the bad and cause trouble, but helping along the good through positive persuasion and creating peace between people may be looked at in a negative way. I don't think so. Creating peace is never a negative concept. And if anyone tells you it is, please don't believe it. Instead, find something good about that person. Then tell someone else.

17

When You Are Allowed to Speak About Others

Make yourself necessary to somebody.

Ralph Waldo Emerson

To the Source

National revelation had taken place at Mount Sinai, but after God spoke the first two commandments, it was too much for the Jewish people, so they sent Moses to receive the commandments on their behalf. They knew he would be back in forty days, but as time went on, they panicked.

The people saw that Moses had delayed in descending the mountain, and the people gathered around Aaron and said to him, "Rise up, make for us gods that will go before us, for this man Moses who brought us up from the land of Egypt—we do not know what became of him!" [55]

And so, just days after being told by God Himself not to worship idols (second of the ten commandments), the people gather and build a golden calf.

Back on Mount Sinai, God does not have good words to say to Moses about the Jewish people:

God spoke to Moses: "Go, descend—for your people that you brought up from the land of Egypt have become corrupt. They have strayed quickly from the way that I have commanded them. They have made themselves a molten calf, prostrated themselves to it and sacrificed to it, and they said, 'This is your god, O Israel, which brought you up from the land of Egypt.'" God said to Moses, "I have seen this people and behold! It is a stiff-necked people."[56]

Hmm. . . . It doesn't seem that God had very nice things to say about the Jewish people. Isn't this a transgression of the laws of positive speech? Aside from the fact that God can do anything He wants, the answer is still "not at all," for as we will see, you are allowed to speak about someone, even it reflects negatively, if there is a constructive and positive purpose. In this case, God wanted Moses to go down to the base of Mount Sinai and get the people to change their ways. He wasn't just gossiping idly about them to Moses—there was a clear reason—and with a clear reason, one is not only allowed to speak, but is obligated to do so.

I saved this chapter until almost the end of this book, because Maimonides says that if you're trying to break a bad habit or character trait, you should first go to the opposite extreme, and that you will eventually make the breakthrough and find the happy medium.

For example, if you are working on anger, make the decision to go for seven days never losing your temper. It's extreme, but it will help you develop your character to the point where you will almost never lose it.

The same with gossip and other forms of destructive speech. This book has been devoted to sensitizing you to the importance of using the gift of speech properly. Now I can tell you, as in the Biblical example above, that there are times when not only are you allowed to speak about people when it reflects badly on them, you are actually *obligated* to.

The overriding rule is that you may have no bad feelings

toward the person, and every word must be for a positive, constructive purpose.

There is a big difference between the following scenarios:

Scenario 1: *Karen finds out that a couple she knows is getting a divorce, and she runs home to tell her husband about it, including all the terrible details.*

Scenario 2: *Karen finds out that a couple she and her husband know are getting a divorce, and when she arrives home she tells her husband that their friends are having marital troubles. "Perhaps you could talk to them, counsel them—I think it could make a difference."*

In both scenarios, a couple's private marital business is being discussed, but clearly there is a marked difference between the two. The first entertains gossip for no other purpose than feeding the sick pleasure of those talking and listening. In the latter, the purpose is to help.

If you are 100 percent clear that what you are about to discuss has a positive purpose, and the information you have is 100 percent accurate, and there is more than a reasonable chance this person can help you with the situation, only then may you say it.

But be careful—don't use this as an open excuse to say whatever you want. Make sure every word has a purpose. This doesn't give you license to open up every detail of a situation. Just say what needs to be said, and be finished.

Ideally, if you can state the information without using names, that's even better. I can sometimes ask my husband's advice about a situation, perhaps regarding counseling I gave to a woman about her marriage, without even saying who it is.

If for some reason the only way my husband can help is by knowing who I am talking about, then I will obtain permission to share names. But again, it doesn't mean I can share every word and detail that were exchanged. Only pertinent information that allows my husband to understand and give advice is allowed.

Evaluate the situation by asking yourself if there is a positive, constructive purpose to your saying something to a third party. Can this person really help, or are you just speaking badly for no purpose at all?

Another good indicator is to ask yourself this: "Am I getting pleasure from discussing this?" If the answer is yes, perhaps your motives are not so pure after all.

Another important example of when you are allowed to talk about people, even if it reflects badly, is when two people are contemplating a partnership, whether it's in business or marriage.

If someone tells you they want to know what you think about them going into business with Mr. Jones, and you know for a fact that Mr. Jones has just been indicted for racketeering, then it is right to say so.

If Jane tells you she is thinking about marrying Larry and wants to know what you think, and you know for a fact that Larry has been married seven times before, you are allowed to share that information.

But be careful—know the difference between fact and opinion.

My husband had been studying Judaism for a few months with a bachelor businessman, who I will call Joe. He told me that Joe really wanted to get married, and he asked me to set

Joe up with some nice girls. I obliged and set Joe up on a date with someone. After the date, the woman called and told me, "It was the date from hell." I felt terrible, and I told my husband what had happened. "That's hard to believe. It must have been a personality mismatch," he said. "Let's set him up with somebody else."

So I did. The next woman he went out with called me after the date and, unbelievably, said the exact same thing! "It was the date from hell."

By this time I was really spooked and totally embarrassed in front of these two young women. I told my husband, "Something is wrong with this guy, and I don't care what you say, I am not setting him up again."

Lo and behold, six months later he is engaged, and to a wonderful woman we know. If that woman had called me up to ask my opinion about this guy, what do you think I would have said? Luckily I never did, and a big lesson was learned: One woman's date from hell is another woman's Prince Charming.

Everyone has opinions. Keep them to yourself. Unless you have clear, concrete evidence of something and sharing it has a clear, positive, constructive purpose (and you have thought about it long and hard), don't say it! If you do, lives can be ruined. Just try taking it back—a feather here, a feather there, a feather, a feather, everywhere.

Before she understood the laws clearly, a friend of mine had the following experience:

Someone called me up and said she knew of a young girl who might be a match for a young boy I knew. She said, "Tell me about him." So, thinking this is one of the times you are allowed to speak about someone, I proceeded to tell her everything I knew, from his past relationships to his therapy. After I was finished, she seemed perplexed.

"Oh," she said, "I just wanted to know how tall he was, because the girl is tall."

I, of course, felt two inches tall.

Now when someone says, "Tell me about him," I answer, "What would you like to know?" And depending on what it is, I can decide if the question is proper to respond to or not.

Remember, people can change. Information about a person's past that no longer applies to them does not have to be shared. Be careful and consult someone more familiar with the laws of speech so you can make the right choice.

If you are not sure if what you are about to say is destructive, then don't say it! Wait, think about it, ask someone more knowledgeable than you in the laws of speech if it is permissible. And be careful—don't speak badly about others while asking. Don't use names of people when you are describing the situation. Just describe it in such a way that they can help you know if you are allowed to speak about it or not.

Again—when in doubt, don't say it. You can always say it later if you are sure it is not destructive speech. Once you say it—you guessed it—it's feathers in the wind. Just try and retrieve 'em.

Those who never retract their opinions love themselves more than they love truth.

Joseph Joubert

18

The Best
Story Ever

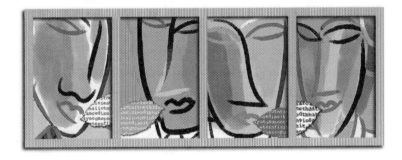

When you have spoken the word, it reigns over you.
When it is unspoken, you reign over it.

Proverb

Toward the end of a speaking engagement in Toronto on the subject of positive speech, a woman I knew raised her hand and asked if she could share a story about something that had happened to her. This is what she said:

I am Jewish. And although I was not raising my three sons in a particularly observant way, after their teens two of them decided to study in Israel and were becoming quite observant. This alarmed my husband and me, so we traveled there to see what was going on.

Thankfully, not only did our sons seem happy and fulfilled, but we were very impressed with the staff and administration of the Judaic college they were attending. They took me to some of the classes, including some that explained the laws of speech. After awhile my husband and I had had enough of the studies and decided to "escape" to the resort town of Netanya.

The first morning there I was lounging by the pool and enjoying the sun. To my left was a woman, also relaxing. To my right were two women who were engaged in an animated conversation. Since I was right beside them I couldn't help but overhear their discussion. They were talking about someone they knew who had just gotten married. They were saying that his first marriage had ended in a very messy way, but they were not sure of the details.

Amazingly, by listening to them I realized that I knew who they were talking about! This guy had grown up with my boys in our community back home! What a small world. And not only that, I happened to know all the details of his first marriage and messy divorce. (An in-the-know friend had filled me in.) I took off my sunglasses and was leaning over with glee, about to tell all, when suddenly a picture of my boys in Jerusalem flashed before me. All those classes on morals and ethics, especially the ones on speech, came swirling through my mind.

You can imagine that it took all my self-control to put my glasses back on, lie back and not say a word. After awhile they finished their talk, got up and left.

A few minutes later the woman to my left asked me the time and we started chatting. We played some "Jewish Geography," and it seemed we had some common friends back home. Then she told me her name, and I swear to you as I am standing here today, it turned out that this woman was the mother of the man's first wife! The man that those two women on my right side had been talking about!

I was stunned, realizing that if I had leaned over and joined that conversation and contributed all the dirt on his first marriage, this woman would surely have overheard. I could picture her standing up and announcing that it was her daughter we were gossiping about. And I would have died a thousand deaths.

This was going through my mind as I nodded and pretended to listen to her. All the while I was thanking my boys and the rabbis in Jerusalem for saving me from what would have been the greatest embarrassment of my life.

As the saying goes, what goes around comes around. So do yourself and so many others a favor: Don't even let it go.

AFTERWORD: ACTIONS SPEAK LOUDER THAN DESIRES

You will become as small as your controlling desire,
as great as your dominant aspiration.

James Allen

As you begin refraining more and more from speaking badly of others, you'll notice that you still may *desire* to speak it, in spite of this dramatic improvement in your character. Know that that's okay, as long as you don't give in to your temptation. The assurance we'd like to give you, however, goes even deeper than that. Not only do we suggest you not feel guilty for still desiring to gossip, we suggest that you feel proud of yourself for desiring to—and still not doing it.

Why? Well, two reasons, really. It is asked in *Ethics of Our Fathers,* "Who is mighty?" The answer? "One who can control his inclinations." Thus, having the inclination, while uncomfortable, is certainly not a sin. But not giving in to your inclination is something to be extremely proud of.

The second reason can be demonstrated through the following story:

A gentleman who had struggled with a weight problem for many years finally found a health program he could live with. His weight steadily decreased and he was now looking and feeling better than ever before. Everyone close to him was proud of him for his efforts and he was justifiably proud of himself. His biggest challenge, however, was that he never did quite lose his sweet tooth—that almost overwhelming desire to sink his teeth into every chocolate cake, ice-cream sundae and jelly donut that crossed his path. He couldn't help feeling a bit guilty about these desires. After all, wasn't he pleased with his progress? Didn't he feel proud of all he had accomplished? Is there something wrong with me, *he asked himself,* for allowing these inclinations to cloud my mind? He even *thought,* Shouldn't I detest the very thought of sweets?

His friend, however, paraphrased—for his current situation—a wise piece of advice he had learned while studying the famous Jewish sage known as "Rashi."

"One should not say 'I do not like to eat sweets,' but rather, 'I do desire them, yet what can I do, since eating them is bad for me?'"

The same dictum could be applied to gossip. For instance, one should not say, "I do not like to gossip," but rather, "I really enjoy talking about and listening to intimate details of other people's lives, and discussing other people's character flaws, but what can I do, since my heavenly Father has forbidden it?"

The bonus is that, once you stop gossiping, the desire to do so also begins to fade. The desire to gossip may not change overnight, but the desire to change can.

As we end, please know that this book has been a labor of

love for us. We're also proud of you for caring enough about improving your life, as well as the lives of those you love and those with whom you come in contact, that you'd take the time to read this book all the way to the end. Now, if you'd like, go back and review any notes you've written or parts you've underlined or highlighted. Review them as often as you'd like and chart your progress.

Here's one piece of advice that we'd like to leave you: If you find yourself slipping, don't get down on yourself and, most of all, don't give up. Instead, be happy with your efforts. Take encouragement every time you think of gossiping and don't. Be delighted every time you want to say something destructive but refrain. And take pleasure every time you catch yourself just before uttering a negative phrase.

It's difficult, we know. When you hold back, no one is there to applaud you. Those around you have no idea that you were just tempted to gossip but didn't. You had the strength to do the right thing. You know you did it, and God knows you did it. And that, dear reader, is amazing.

Don't be discouraged by small failures but, instead, build on your small successes.

To life!

Lori Palatnik and Bob Burg

It is much easier to suppress a first desire than to satisfy those that follow.

François de La Rochefoucauld

APPENDIX: THE TEN PATHWAYS OF POSITIVE SPEECH

Better pointed bullets than pointed speech.

Otto von Bismarck

The Ten Pathways of Positive Speech

1. Speak No Evil. *Say only positive statements. Let words of kindness be on your tongue.*
2. Hear No Evil. *Refuse to listen to gossip, slander and other negative forms of speech.*
3. Don't Rationalize Destructive Speech. *Excuses like "But it's true" or "I'm only joking" or "I can tell my spouse anything" just don't cut it.*
4. See No Evil. *Judge people favorably, the way you would want them to judge you.*
5. Beware of Speaking Evil Without Saying an Evil Word. *Body language and even positive speech can bring tremendous destruction.*
6. Be Humble; Avoid Arrogance. *These will be your greatest weapons against destructive speech.*

7. Beware of Repeating Information. *Loose lips sink ships. Even positive information needs permission before being repeated.*

8. Honesty Really Is the Best Policy—Most of the Time. *Be careful to always tell the truth, unless it will hurt others, break your own privacy or publicize your accomplishments.*

9. Learn to Say "I'm Sorry." *Everyone makes mistakes. If you've spoken badly about someone, clear it up immediately.*

10. Forgive. *If you have been wronged, let it go.*

NOTES

1. Deuteronomy 30:15—19.
2. Genesis 1:3.
3. Genesis 1:6.
4. Genesis 1:26.
5. Ibid.
6. See "Targum Onkelos" on Genesis 2:7.
7. Jewish mysticism.
8. *Ethics of Our Fathers* 1:15.
9. *Ethics of Our Fathers* 2:21.
10. Exodus 3:4.
11. Exodus 3:6.
12. Exodus 3:12.
13. Exodus 3:16.
14. Exodus 3:18.
15. Exodus 4:6—7.
16. Numbers 12:10—15.
17. Kosher food laws that apply to Jews and prohibit the mixing or eating of certain foods, including pork.
18. Talmud Bavli, Sanhedrin, 74a.
19. Babylonian Talmud, Arachin 15b.
20. Exodus 13:25—26.
21. Ibid.
22. Exodus 14:1—3.
23. Sefer HaChinuch, commandment 240.
24. Genesis 37:2.
25. Genesis 37:4.
26. Mishnah Torah, Book of Knowledge, Laws of Character Development, 7:2.
27. *Ethics of Our Fathers* 4:17.
28. *Ethics of Our Fathers* 3:17.
29. Genesis 50:15—17.
30. Samuel 1:10—17.
31. Ibid.
32. *Ethics of Our Fathers* 2:5.
33. Irving M. Bunim, *Ethics from Sinai,* New York: Feldheim, 1964, commenting on *Ethics of Our Fathers* 2:5.
34. Babylonian Talmud, Pesachim 113b.
35. Yad, Teshuvah 3:2.
36. Leviticus 19:18.
37. Genesis 29:4—6.
38. Numbers 16:3.
39. Numbers 16:5—7.
40. Exodus 6:10.
41. Genesis 2:15—17.
42. Genesis 3:1.
43. Babylonian Talmud, Chulin 89a.
44. Babylonian Talmud, Shabbos 55a.
45. Genesis 18:12—13.
46. Babylonian Talmud, Baba Metzia 23b.
47. Babylonian Talmud, Kesuvos 17b.
48. Babylonian Talmud, Eruvin 13b.
49. Genesis 4:2—6.
50. Genesis 4:8—9.
51. Yad, Teshuva 2:2.
52. Genesis 45:4—8.
53. Genesis 45:9—11.
54. Psalms 34:15.
55. Exodus 32:1.
56. Exodus 32:7—9.

FURTHER READING

Adahan, Dr. Miriam. *Sticks and Stones*. Jerusalem: Feldheim Publishers, 1998.

Burg, Bob. *Winning Without Intimidation*. Jupiter, FL: Samark, 1998.

Palatnik, Lori. *Remember My Soul*. Pikesville, MD: Leviathan Press, 1998.

Pliskin, Rabbi Zelig. *Guard Your Tongue*. Brooklyn, NY: Benei Yaakov Publications, 1975.

———. *The Power of Words*. Brooklyn, NY: Benei Yaakov Publications, 1988.

Rich, Hillary, Katzoff, Irwin, and Feld, Chaim. *The Words Can Heal Handbook*. Pikesville, MD: Leviathan Press, 2001.

Samet, Yehudis. *The Other Side of the Story: Giving People the Benefit of the Doubt*. Brooklyn, NY: Mesorah Publications, LTD/Artscroll, 1996.

Telushkin, Rabbi Joseph. *Words Can Hurt, Words Can Heal*. New York: Quill, 1998.

———. *The Book of Jewish Values*. New York: Bell Tower, 2000.

ABOUT THE AUTHORS

Lori Palatnik is an author and Jewish educator. She has been a guest on numerous radio and television talk shows, and hosted a Toronto television show called "The Jewish Journal." She lectures on the beauty and depth of Judaism throughout the United States and Israel, and has written articles on Jewish topics for *The Jerusalem Report, Toronto Star* and many other publications. Lori is the author of *Friday Night and Beyond—The Shabbat Experience Step-by-Step* and *Remember My Soul.* She recently relocated with her husband, Rabbi Yaakov Palatnik, to Denver, Colorado, and is the mother of five children.

Bob Burg is an internationally known speaker and author. He has spoken to Fortune 500 companies, associations and individuals on topics related to business networking and positive persuasion. He has been featured on the national rally circuit, sharing the platform with legends such as Zig Ziglar, Larry King, Mark Victor Hansen, Willard Scott, Paul Harvey, Mary Lou Retton, Lou Holtz, Gerald Ford and many others. A frequent media guest, Bob's articles have also been published in hundreds of professional and trade magazines. His books include *Endless Referrals: Network Your Everyday Contacts into Sales* and *Winning Without Intimidation: How to Master the Art of Positive Persuasion.* He lives in Jupiter, Florida, and may be reached at *www.burg.com*, where you can also subscribe to his free weekly e-mail newsletter.

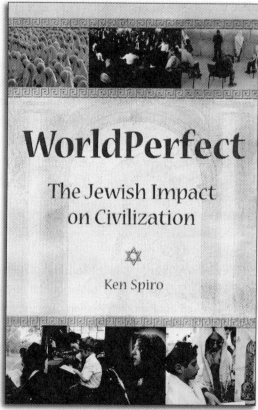